WORD ROOTS

B1

LEARNING THE BUILDING BLOCKS
OF BETTER SPELLING AND VOCABULARY

Word Roots Series
📖 Beginning 📖 A1 📖 A2 📖 B1 📖 B2
Flashcards: Beginning • A1 • A2 • B1

Written by
Cherie A. Plant

Graphic Design by
Annette Langenstein

Edited by
Patricia Gray
Alane Jennings

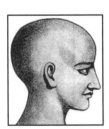

© 2011, 2002
THE CRITICAL THINKING CO.™
www.CriticalThinking.com
Phone: 800-458-4849 • Fax: 831-393-3277
P.O. Box 1610 • Seaside • CA 93955-1610
ISBN 978-0-89455-805-4

SUSTAINABLE FORESTRY INITIATIVE   Certified Sourcing
www.sfiprogram.org
Label applies to the text stock   SFI-00341

TABLE OF CONTENTS

INTRODUCTION

"To be a power one must know how to use language;
and how can you place words together unless you know
their derivation and their real meaning?"

—Henry Kraeme

Word Roots is designed to help students expand their spelling, vocabulary, and comprehension skills. *Word Roots* is a uniquely designed and challenging workbook based on the word elements: roots, prefixes, and suffixes. Note that the roots used in this book originate from the Greek language – the foundation of much of our English language.

Roots, prefixes, and suffixes are the building blocks upon which all words are formed. A thorough knowledge of these elements will greatly enhance one's vocabulary and improve one's understanding of otherwise unfamiliar words. For example, understanding the meaning of **scop**, **phon**, **tele**, **peri**, and **meter** would enable one to comprehend many words made from combinations of these elements, such as the following:

telephone	phonic	periscopic	telescope
telemetry	phonometer	perimeter	periscope
telescopic	telephonic	telemeter	phonoscope

Even more dramatically, the Greek root **hydr** is the basis for some fifty words in our language. The significance of this is revealed in the fact that with every new root learned, the resulting growth of one's vocabulary can be truly astounding – and *Word Roots* provides the tools.

Definitions of Root, Prefix, and Suffix

A **root** is the element that gives the basic meaning of the word. In this book, the term root refers to the original Greek* word. An English word may have two or more roots in it. Identifying these roots can help you to define a word you don't know.

A **prefix** is an element that is added to the beginning of a word. The prefix adds to or alters the meaning of the basic word. For example, the prefix **ant-** means opposite. The root **onym** means word.

> ant + onym = antonym means a word that is opposite in meaning

The prefix **syn-** means with or together.

> syn + onym = synonym means a word that is similar in meaning

A **suffix** is an element added to the end of a word. The suffix modifies the meaning of the basic word.

Root: **dermato** = skin   Suffixes: **-logy** (study of, science), **-ist** (one who), **-ic** (like, related to)

> dermato + logy = dermatology means the study of skin
>
> dermato + logy + ist = dermatologist means one who studies skin
>
> dermato + logy + ic = dermatologic means related to the study of skin

*Note: In this book, all roots are Greek in origin. Prefixes and suffixes may be either Latin or Greek.

How to Do the Activities

The worksheets help the student to meet several objectives. Given Latin and Greek elements and their definitions, the student will:

1. Identify these elements in English words.
2. Match each given word to its correct meaning.
3. Select the correct word to complete an unfinished sentence.

Identifying the Elements

The information below will help the student identify the word elements (Objective 1 above).

- A word can have more than one root, as shown below. Each root is circled.

  thermo + meter = (thermo)(meter)

- In some words, connecting vowels and/or consonants are used to join word parts or to complete a word. For the sake of simplicity, connecting vowels and consonants used to join word parts or to complete words will appear in gray.

  herb + i + cide = herbicide
  fer + t + ile = fertile
  medi + at + or = mediator
  de + scribe = describe

- In some cases, to help smooth the sound of the spoken word, a vowel is added to a root. This vowel (usually an o), is referred to as a connecting vowel, and the modified root is called a combining form. For example, the root **hydr** uses the connecting vowel o to produce the combining form **hydro,** which then combines with the root **electr** and the suffix -ic to form the word **hydroelectric**. In the lessons, an asterisk (*) is used to indicate if a root is a combining form.

  hydr + o = hydro (combining form)
  hydro + electr + ic = hydroelectric

Some roots are considered to be combining forms, yet do not follow the general rule.

- The last letter may be dropped when a suffix is added.

  dermato + logy + ist   -**logy** drops the y in (dermato)logist

- Variations in the spelling of roots are given when necessary. For example, **therm** or **thermo** are both forms of the same Latin root. When both forms are used, the root is listed with its alternatives.

Completing the Exercises

Each worksheet has a 3-column box listing the word elements used on the page and their definitions. A prefix ends with a hyphen (-) indicating that text follows; a suffix begins with a hyphen indicating that text precedes it.

Focus Elements

Each worksheet is labeled at the top with a focus element(s) for that page. Every word in Column A uses at least one focus element. Non-focus elements used in the words in Column A are also shown in the prefix, root, or suffix list. Pages 51–54 do not have a focus element, but each word is formed with a combination of roots.

The student should do each worksheet as instructed below:

1. Study the meanings of the prefixes, roots, and suffixes given.

2. In Column A, identify the Greek and Latin elements used in each word by circling roots and underlining prefixes and suffixes.

3. For each word in Column A, write the letter of the correct meaning from Column B. For words taken from a specific subject, such as biology or botany, the subject is listed in parentheses after the definition.

4. Use the words from Column A to complete the sentences. Write or underline the best word to complete each sentence.

PARTIAL SAMPLE WORKSHEET

FOCUS: phon/phono

PREFIX		ROOT		SUFFIX	
sym-	with, together	phob	fear of	-ia	condition
		phon/ phono	sound	-ic	like, related to
		poly*	many		

DIRECTIONS: In Column A, identify the elements in each word by circling roots and underlining prefixes and suffixes. Then match each word with its correct meaning from column B.

COLUMN A

1. sym(phon)ic   _b_
2. (phono)(phob)ia   _c_
3. (poly)(phon)ic   _a_

COLUMN B

a. having many sounds
b. having the same sound
c. fear of sound or speaking

DIRECTIONS: Choose the best word from Column A for each sentence. Use each word only once.

1. The woman's ___phonophobia___ made her avoid busy locations like the mall.

2. The quartet performed a ___symphonic___ piece.

3. In a ___polyphonic___ composition, each voice has its own distinct melody.

Extension Worksheets

Extension activities, starting on page 55, can be used for assessment or additional practice. There are three extension activities for each group of exercises. Worksheets One, Two, and Three review the words introduced on pages 1–12; Worksheets Four, Five, and Six review pages 13–24; Worksheets Seven, Eight, and Nine review pages 25–37; and Worksheets Ten, Eleven, and Twelve review pages 38–50. Worksheet 13 includes words from the whole book.

PRETEST/POSTTEST

 Before starting *Word Roots*, test your existing knowledge of word meanings. On the blank spaces provided, write what you think the following words mean. However, do not score your answers at this time. After you complete the book, take the test again, and then score your answers. Compare your answers from before and after to determine the progress you've made.

1. gynarchy _____

2. autocosm _____

3. pericardial _____

4 autonomous _____

5. misanthrope _____

6. hypothermia _____

7. synchronous _____

8. mesocracy _____

9. eulogy _____

10. genocide _____

11. somatology _____

12. pathogenic _____

13. macrobiosis _____

14. kleptomania _____

15. micrometer _____

16. monotheism _____

17. xenophile _____

18. hydrophobia _____

19. antisymmetric _____

20. polychrome _____

WARM-UP ACTIVITY: THINKING ABOUT MEANING

DIRECTIONS: Use the meanings of the given elements to define each word. (Roots are Greek, prefixes and suffixes are Latin or Greek.) The first has been done for you.

1. **arthritis** = arthr + itis (root, suffix)
   arthr means joint; **-itis** means inflammation

   Then *arthritis* means <u>inflammation of the joint</u>

2. **pseudonym** = pseud + onym (root, root)
   pseud means false; **onym** means name, word

   Then pseudonym means _____

3. **euthanasia** = eu + thanas + ia (prefix, root, suffix)
   eu- means good or well; **thanas** means death; **-ia** means condition.

   Then e*uthanasia* means _____

4. **acrophobia** = acro + phob + ia (root, root, suffix)
   acro means height, top, extremity; **phob** means fear; **-ia** means condition.

   Then *acrophobia* means _____

5. **geographer** = geo + graph + er (root, root, suffix)
   geo means earth, ground; **graph** means write, written; **-er** means one who, that which

   Then *geographer* means _____

6. **bicentric** = bi + centr + ic (prefix, root, suffix)
   bi- means two; **centr** means center; **-ic** means like, related to

   Then *bicentric* means _____

7. **geopathology** = geo + patho + logy (root, root, suffix)
   geo means earth, ground; **patho** means feeling, disease; **-logy** means study of, science

   Then *geopathology* means _____

FOCUS: chrom/chrome/chromo

PREFIX		ROOT		SUFFIX	
hyper-	over, above	**chrom/**	color	**-ia**	condition
hypo-	under, below	**chrome/**		**-ic**	like, related to
mono-	one	**chromo**		**-ium**	chemical element
		gen	cause, birth, race, produce		
		poly*	many		
		scope	look at, view, examine		

DIRECTIONS: In Column A, identify the elements in each word by circling roots and underlining prefixes and suffixes. Then match each word with its correct meaning from Column B.

COLUMN A

1. (chrom)(gen)ic ____
2. chromium ____
3. chromoscope ____
4. hyperchromia ____
5. hypochromia ____
6. monochrome ____
7. polychrome ____

COLUMN B

a. lack of color
b. optical instrument used to study various properties of color, including value and intensity
c. excessive pigmentation (color), as of the skin
d. many-colored
e. element used for making pigments
f. made of shades of a single color
g. producing color

DIRECTIONS: Choose the best word from Column A for each sentence. Use each word only once.

1. Early photography produced a _____ image.

2. The fluid contained a _____ substance which caused it to turn green.

3. The technician used a portable _____ to analyze the paint on the car.

4. _____ is a hard metal used in photographic compounds.

5. The _____ vase contained shades of red, blue, and yellow.

6. Aging skin is often affected with _____.

7. The rare white rhinoceros is an animal that exhibits _____.

*For more information, please refer to the Introduction.

FOCUS: derm

PREFIX		ROOT		SUFFIX	
epi-	on, outside	**derm**	skin	**-al**	like, related to; an action or process
hypo-	under, below	**meso***	middle	**-ic**	like, related to
		pachy	thick	**-oid**	resembling

DIRECTIONS: In Column A, identify the elements in each word by circling roots and underlining prefixes and suffixes. Then match each word with its correct meaning from Column B.

COLUMN A

1. epi(derm)al   ____
2. dermoid   ____
3. hypodermic   ____
4. mesodermic   ____
5. pachyderm   ____

COLUMN B

a. resembling skin (Medical)
b. under the skin
c. related to the middle layer of skin (Biology)
d. related to the outer layer of skin (Biology)
e. mammal with thick skin

DIRECTIONS: Choose the best word from Column A for each sentence. Use each word only once.

1. The rhinoceros and the elephant are each examples of a _____ .

2. A _____ tumor or cyst often appears on the face.

3. The nurse gave the patient a _____ injection to ease his pain.

4. A snake sheds its _____ layer to reveal new skin below.

5. The knife cut through the outer layers of tissue but didn't affect the _____ tissue.

*For more information, please refer to the Introduction.

FOCUS: chron/chrono

PREFIX		ROOT		SUFFIX	
ana-	back, against	**chron/ chrono**	time	**-al**	like, related to; an action or process
syn-	with, together	**geo**	earth, ground	**-ic**	like, related to
		meter	measure	**-ism**	act, state, condition
		therm	heat	**-logy**	study of, science
				-ous	having the quality of

DIRECTIONS: In Column A, identify the elements in each word by circling roots and underlining prefixes and suffixes. Then match each word with its correct meaning from Column B.

COLUMN A

1. ana(chron)ism ____
2. geochronology ____
3. synchronous ____
4. chronothermal ____
5. chronic ____
6. chronology ____
7. chronometer ____

COLUMN B

a. continuing a long time or recurring frequently
b. timekeeping device of great accuracy, especially used in measuring longitude
c. occurring at the same time
d. science of determining the order in which things occur
e. something out of place or time
f. relating to both time and temperature
g. study of the ages of geologic events

DIRECTIONS: Choose the best word from Column A for each sentence. Use each word only once.

1. Because of her _____ arthritis, the elderly woman was in constant pain.

2. An astronaut living in the eighteenth century would be a/an _____.

3. Historians try to determine an accurate _____ of events during a period.

4. Scientists use _____ to pinpoint various stages of the earth's development.

5. The _____ equation could be used even though the specimen became several degrees colder over the two hours.

6. Both performers were prepared to start so their acts would be _____.

7. The measurements of the early versions of the _____ were affected by the motion of the ship.

FOCUS: bi/bio, ops/opt/opto

PREFIX		ROOT		SUFFIX	
syn-	with, together	bi/ bio	life	-al	like, related to; an action or process
		gen	cause, birth, produce, race	-ic	like, related to
		metr	measure	-y	state of, quality, act; body, group
		ops/ opt/ opto	eye, vision		
		phone	sound		

DIRECTIONS: In Column A, identify the elements in each word by circling roots and underlining prefixes and suffixes. Then match each word with its correct meaning from Column B.

COLUMN A   COLUMN B

1. (opto)(metr)y _____   a. removal and examination of tissue from a living body (Medical)

2. synoptic _____   b. device used by the visually impaired to convert written text into sounds

3. optical _____   c. related to statistical analysis of biological observations and phenomena

4. optophone _____   d. testing of eyes to measure vision

5. biopsy _____   e. produced by the action of living organisms

6. biometric _____   f. pertaining to the eye; vision

7. biogenic _____   g. taking a general view of the whole subject

DIRECTIONS: Choose the best word from Column A for each sentence. Use each word only once.

1. The medical student decided to pursue a career in _____.

2. The results of the _____ indicated that there were no cancer cells.

3. M.C. Escher was an artist who distorted perspective in order to create an _____ illusion.

4. The teacher used the _____ to provide materials for her students who did not read Braille.

5. _____ sediments found along the coast include skeletons and shells.

6. The doctor gave a _____ presentation of the patient's condition after reviewing all the files.

7. He completed _____ research on the behavior patterns of gypsy moths.

FOCUS: therm/thermo

PREFIX	ROOT		SUFFIX	
hypo- under, below	**chrono**	time	**-al**	like, related to; an action or process
	gen	cause, birth, produce, race	**-ia**	condition
	geo	earth, ground	**-ic**	like, related to
	graph	write, written	**-y**	state of, quality, act; body, group
	meter	measure		
	therm/ thermo	heat		

DIRECTIONS: In Column A, identify the elements in each word by circling roots and underlining prefixes and suffixes. Then match each word with its correct meaning from Column B.

COLUMN A

1. chronothermal ____
2. geothermal ____
3. thermometer ____
4. hypothermia ____
5. thermal ____
6. thermography ____
7. thermogenic ____

COLUMN B

a. condition of reduced temperature

b. relating to both time and temperature

c. of or related to heat; caused by heat

d. recording a visual image of body heat using infrared devices (Medical)

e. producing heat (Physiology)

f. instrument which measures heat

g. related to the heat of the earth's interior

DIRECTIONS: Choose the best word from Column A for each sentence. Use each word only once.

1. The mother used a _____ to check her child's temperature.

2. A change in temperature over time is a _____ phenomenon.

3. The swimmer remained in the cold water so long he suffered from _____.

4. He used a _____ sensor to detect areas of heat loss in the house.

5. _____ is used in scanning breast tissue for possible tumors.

6. Numerous companies market _____ weight loss products that will burn fat.

7. Homes in Iceland are heated using _____ power stations.

FOCUS: hydr/hydro

PREFIX		ROOT		SUFFIX	
de-	from, away, down, apart; not	**gen**	cause, birth, race, produce	**-al**	like, related to; an action or process
		geo	earth, ground	**-ant**	one who, that which; state, quality
		graph	write, written		
		hydr/ hydro*	water	**-ate**	to make, to act; one who, that which
		onym	name, word	**-ic**	like, related to
		path	feeling, disease	**-logy**	study of, science
		phone	sound	**-y**	state of, quality, act; body, group
		therm	heat		

DIRECTIONS: In Column A, identify the elements in each word by circling roots and underlining prefixes and suffixes. Then match each word with its correct meaning from Column B.

COLUMN A

1. de(hydr)ate ____
2. hydrant ____
3. hydrothermal ____
4. hydrogenic ____
5. hydrophone ____
6. hydrogeology ____
7. hydropathy ____
8. hydrograph ____
9. hydronymy ____

COLUMN B

a. of or related to hot water

b. naming or names of bodies of water (History)

c. receiver for listening to sound transmitted through water

d. treatment of injury or disease with water (Medical)

e. diagram of the levels or amount of water flow in a river

f. device for drawing water

g. caused by the action of water (Geology)

h. to take water from

i. study of subsurface water movement through rocks

DIRECTIONS: Choose the best word from Column A for each sentence. Use each word only once.

1. Firefighters were forced to let the building burn for lack of a/an _____.

2. The navy ship used a/an _____ to detect the submarine.

3. Geologists attributed the erosion of the hillsides to _____ forces.

4. You can _____ fruits and vegetables using a microwave.

5. The _____ indicated the winter runoff was minimal.

6. Soaking in a _____ bath relieved his tension.

7. Trainers have long been aware of the benefits of _____ for injured athletes.

8. The _____ of an area is often influenced by native cultures.

9. The source of underground streams can be identified using _____.

FOCUS: andr/andro

PREFIX	ROOT		SUFFIX	
	andr/ **andro***	man, male	**-ic**	like, related to
	centr	center	**-oid**	resembling
	crac	government, rule	**-ous**	having the quality of
	gen	cause, birth, race, produce	**-y**	state of, quality, act; body group
	gyn	woman, female		
	poly*	many		

DIRECTIONS: In Column A, identify the elements in each word by circling roots and underlining prefixes and suffixes. Then match each word with its correct meaning from Column B.

COLUMN A

1. (andr)oid   _____
2. polyandry   _____
3. androgynous   _____
4. androcentric   _____
5. androgen   _____
6. androcracy   _____

COLUMN B

a. having both male and female characteristics.

b. male sex hormone

c. humanlike robot

d. political and social rule by men

e. centered around male interests

f. the practice of having two or more husbands at one time

DIRECTIONS: Choose the best word from Column A for each sentence. Use each word only once.

1. _____ is illegal in the United States.

2. In an _____ society, women are subservient to men.

3. _____ has been the norm historically in most countries.

4. In its outward appearance, the _____ was remarkably lifelike.

5. Her short haircut and baggy clothes gave her an _____ appearance.

6. Testosterone is a well known _____.

FOCUS: auto

PREFIX	ROOT		SUFFIX	
	auto*	self	**-ous**	having the quality of
	bio	life	**-y**	state of, quality, act; body, group
	cosm	universe, harmony		
	crac	government, rule		
	gen	cause, birth, race, produce		
	graph	write, written		
	nom	name, law, custom, order		

DIRECTIONS: In Column A, identify the elements in each word by circling roots and underlining prefixes and suffixes. Then match each word with its correct meaning from Column B.

COLUMN A

1. auto crac y _____
2. autograph _____
3. autocosm _____
4. autonomous _____
5. autogenous _____
6. autobiography _____

COLUMN B

a. produced from within; self-generating
b. person's life history written by himself
c. rule by one person with unlimited power
d. person's signature
e. self-created private world
f. self-governing; subject to one's own laws

DIRECTIONS: Choose the best word from Column A for each sentence. Use each word only once.

1. Some animals can repair their own wounds with _____ tissue.

2. They were eager to get the actor's _____ on their programs.

3. A homeowners association is an example of an _____ group.

4. The villagers plotted a rebellion against the _____.

5. The author's _____ was as interesting to read as were her novels.

6. The recluse had retreated into her own _____.

FOCUS: eu-, onym

PREFIX		ROOT		SUFFIX	
an-	not, without	**gen**	cause, birth, race, produce	**-ic**	like, related to
ant-	against, opposite	**hydr**	water	**-ous**	having the quality of
eu-	good, well	**nom**	name, law, custom, order	**-y**	state of, quality, act; body, group
syn-	with, together	**onym**	name, word		
		phon	sound		

DIRECTIONS: In Column A, identify the elements in each word by circling roots and underlining prefixes and suffixes. Then match each word with its correct meaning from Column B.

COLUMN A		COLUMN B
1. eugenic ____		a. of good birth
2. euphony ____		b. word that is opposite in meaning
3. eunomy ____		c. naming or names of bodies of water (History)
4. euonym ____		d. having a similar meaning (Linguistics)
5. onymous ____		e. civil order under good laws; good government
6. anonymous ____		f. well-suited name
7. hydronymy ____		g. having the writer's name
8. synonymous ____		h. pleasing or sweet sound
9. antonym ____		i. without a name

DIRECTIONS: Choose the best word from Column A for each sentence. Use each word only once.

1. Some magazine articles do not state the author's name, but this one is _____.

2. Placing the suffix anti before a word can create an _____.

3. The _____ of the region's lakes and rivers reflects its Celtic heritage.

4. Sunshine was a _____ for our dog because of the joy she brought to us.

5. After receiving the _____ letter, she wondered who had sent it.

6. The audience enjoyed listening to the _____ of the different instruments.

7. Citizens of the kingdom enjoyed a state of _____ during his reign.

8. In medieval times, only those who were _____ could own property.

9. He replaced the difficult word with an easier one that was _____.

FOCUS: mis/miso

PREFIX	ROOT		SUFFIX	
	anthrope	mankind, man	**-ism**	act, state, condition
	gam	united, joined	**-ist**	one who
	gyn	woman, female	**-y**	state of, quality, act;
	log	word, reason		body, group
	mis/	to hate		
	miso*			
	ne	new, recent		

DIRECTIONS: In Column A, identify the elements in each word by circling roots and underlining prefixes and suffixes. Then match each word with its correct meaning from Column B.

COLUMN A

1. misoneism ____
2. misogyny ____
3. misanthrope ____
4. misologist ____
5. misogamist ____

COLUMN B

a. one who hates mankind
b. one who hates reasoning
c. one who hates marriage
d. hatred of women
e. hatred of innovation or change

DIRECTIONS: Choose the best word from Column A for each sentence. Use each word only once.

1. His hostile behavior towards only female staff members revealed his _____.

2. The _____ would not listen to other's arguments, preferring to follow his heart.

3. Neighbors considered him a _____ and left him alone.

4. The _____ had been a bachelor all his life.

5. If a society allows _____ to thrive, that culture may become obsolete.

FOCUS: the/theo

PREFIX		ROOT		SUFFIX	
a-	away, from; not, without	**nom**	name, law, custom, order	**-ism**	act, state, condition
mono-	one	**path**	feeling, disease	**-logy**	study of, science
		poly*	many	**-y**	state of, quality, act; body, group
		psycho	mind, spirit		
		the/	god		
		theo			

DIRECTIONS: In Column A, identify the elements in each word by circling roots and underlining prefixes and suffixes. Then match each word with its correct meaning from Column B.

COLUMN A

1. a(the)ism _____
2. monotheism _____
3. polytheism _____
4. theology _____
5. theopathy _____
6. psychotheism _____
7. theonomy _____

COLUMN B

a. governed by a god; divine rule

b. doctrine that God is pure spirit

c. study of the nature of God

d. intense absorption in religious devotion

e. belief in many gods

f. denial of the existence of a god

g. belief in one god

DIRECTIONS: Choose the best word from Column A for each sentence. Use each word only once.

1. Many rulers have considered their reigns forms of _____.

2. All forms of Christianity practice _____.

3. According to _____, God would possess no physical attributes.

4. Those who practice _____ would not state, "God bless America."

5. People exhibit a form of _____ when they scream and faint during revival meetings.

6. The mythology of Greece and Rome is evidence that they practiced _____.

7. _____ is a major portion of a minister's education.

FOCUS: naut, nom/nomo

PREFIX	ROOT		SUFFIX	
	astro*	star, heavens	**-al**	like, related to; an action or process
	auto*	self	**-er**	one who, that which
	graph	write, written	**-ic**	like, related to
	hydro*	water	**-ics**	science, related to, system
	naut	sailor, ship	**-logy**	study of, science
	nom/	name, law,	**-ous**	having the quality of
	nomo	custom, order	**-y**	state of, quality, act; body, group

DIRECTIONS: In Column A, identify the elements in each word by circling roots and underlining prefixes and suffixes. Then match each word with its correct meaning from Column B.

COLUMN A

1. astronomy _____
2. nomographer _____
3. nomology _____
4. autonomous _____
5. nautical _____
6. hydronautics _____
7. astronaut _____

COLUMN B

a. one who travels throughout the universe

b. self-governing, subject to one's own laws

c. science of laws and lawmaking (Philosophy)

d. technology related to the development of deep submersible vehicles

e. science dealing with the order of celestial bodies

f. related to ships or sailing

g. one who writes laws (History)

DIRECTIONS: Choose the best word from Column A for each sentence. Use each word only once.

1. In ancient Rome, the edicts of the emperor were recorded by a _____.

2. The American colonies fought to be _____ rather than be ruled by England.

3. The discovery of the telescope led to great strides in the field of _____.

4. Neil Armstrong was the first American _____ to walk on the moon.

5. _____ researches how human behavior conforms to rules of conduct.

6. A ship's captain is well trained in _____ procedures.

7. Advances in the field of _____ have enabled scientists to explore the marine canyon in the Monterey Bay.

FOCUS: graph/grapho

PREFIX	ROOT		SUFFIX	
mono- one	**bio**	life	**-logy**	study of, science
	geo	earth, ground	**-y**	state of, quality, act; body, group
	graph/ grapho	write, written		
	macro*	large, great		
	neo*	new, recent		

DIRECTIONS: In Column A, identify the elements in each word by circling roots and underlining prefixes and suffixes. Then match each word with its correct meaning from Column B.

COLUMN A   **COLUMN B**

1. (biograph)y   _____   a. study of handwriting

2. macrograph   _____   b. new system or method of writing

3. graphology   _____   c. description of the earth's features

4. monograph   _____   d. image that is equal to or larger than the object

5. geography   _____   e. written story of someone's life

6. neography   _____   f. detailed scholarly article or book on a single topic

DIRECTIONS: Choose the best word from Column A for each sentence. Use each word only once.

1. I recently read a fascinating _____ of Albert Einstein and his achievements.

2. The continents vary in terms of their _____.

3. The detectives used _____ to determine that the letter had been written by the suspect.

4. The medical journal contained a _____ covering the use of intravenous anesthesia back to 1872.

5. The Arabic _____ gradually replaced Roman numerals.

6. He hung a life-sized _____ of her photo on the wall.

FOCUS: gynec/gyneco, pod/podo

PREFIX	ROOT		SUFFIX	
bi- two	**centr**	center	**-ic**	like, related to
tri- three	**dermat**	skin	**-itis**	inflammation
	gen	cause, birth, race, produce	**-oid**	resembling
	gynec/ gyneco	woman, female	**-logy**	study of, science
	pod/ podo	foot		
	poly*	many		

DIRECTIONS: In Column A, identify the elements in each word by circling roots and underlining prefixes and suffixes. Then match each word with its correct meaning from Column B.

COLUMN A

1. bipod _____
2. podology _____
3. polypod _____
4. tripod _____
5. pododermatitis _____
6. gynecocentric _____
7. gynecology _____
8. gynecogenic _____
9. gynecoid _____

COLUMN B

a. inflammation of skin tissue of the foot
b. causing female characteristics
c. two-legged support
d. centered around the female point of view
e. study of physiology of the feet (Medical)
f. physically resembling the female
g. three-legged stand
h. science of women's disorders (Medical)
i. having many feet

DIRECTIONS: Choose the best word from Column A for each sentence. Use each word only once.

1. The victim was identified as a woman based on the _____ skeletal remains.

2. You would see a doctor who specializes in _____ to treat an ingrown toenail.

3. A portable _____ is a typical part of a photographer's equipment.

4. A physician who specializes in _____ would treat ovarian cancer.

5. The _____ hormone was responsible for the man's feminine voice.

6. A case of _____ can restrict one's ability to walk.

7. A matriarchy is a form of a _____ society.

8. A centipede is an example of a _____ insect.

9. He used a tripod because he needed more stability than a _____ could offer.

FOCUS: psych/psycho

PREFIX	ROOT		SUFFIX	
	bio life		**-ic** like, related to	
	graph write, written		**-logy** study of, science	
	metr measure		**-osis** condition	
	nom name, law, custom, order			
	psych/ mind, spirit			
	psycho			
	somat body			

DIRECTIONS: In Column A, identify the elements in each word by circling roots and underlining prefixes and suffixes. Then match each word with its correct meaning from Column B.

COLUMN A

1. (psycho)(metr)ic ____
2. psychograph ____
3. psychology ____
4. psychosomatic ____
5. psychosis ____
6. psychonomic ____
7. psychobiology ____

COLUMN B

a. study of relationship between biological processes and behavior

b. related to the effect of the mind on the body

c. related to laws of behavior and cognitive function

d. chart of an individual's personality traits

e. science of the mind

f. related to the measurement of mental data

g. condition of mental illness

DIRECTIONS: Choose the best word from Column A for each sentence. Use each word only once.

1. He submitted his article on hallucination to a publication in the field of _____

2. A patient suffering from a _____ may suffer delusions.

3. Hysterical paralysis is a _____ condition.

4. Management reviews each candidate's _____ prior to the interview.

5. The results of _____ testing are often expressed quantitatively rather than qualitatively.

6. A recent publication in _____ research focused on the role of familiarity and meaning in mental transformations.

7. Physicians in the field of _____ are studying the emotional effects of menopause.

FOCUS: astro

PREFIX	ROOT		SUFFIX	
	astro*	star, heavens	**-ics**	science, related to, system
	geo	earth, ground	**-logy**	study of, science
	graph	write, written	**-y**	state of, quality, act; body, group
	metr	measure		
	naut	sailor, ship		
	nom	name, law, custom, order		

DIRECTIONS: In Column A, identify the elements in each word by circling roots and underlining prefixes and suffixes. Then match each word with its correct meaning from Column B.

COLUMN A

1. astronomy _____
2. astrogeology _____
3. astrology _____
4. astrometry _____
5. astrography _____
6. astronautics _____

COLUMN B

a. mapping of the planets and stars
b. measurement of the positions and distances of stars
c. science dealing with the order of celestial bodies
d. study of the structure and composition of heavenly bodies
e. study of the influence of the stars on humans
f. technology of spacecraft design and building

DIRECTIONS: Choose the best word from Column A for each sentence. Use each word only once.

1. The psychic relied on her knowledge of _____ to foretell the future.

2. A specially designed photographic telescope is used in _____ to make charting easier.

3. Sensors aboard the Hubble space telescope help the _____ team measure star positions.

4. Scientists have used _____ to determine that other planets in our solar system are also round.

5. _____ explains the nature and configuration of our solar system.

6. Scientists in the field of _____ will help us to further explore outer space.

FOCUS: biblio, mania

PREFIX	ROOT		SUFFIX	
mono- one	**biblio**	book	**-ia**	condition
	graph/ grapho	write, written	**-logy**	study of, science
	klept/ klepto	to steal	**-y**	state of, quality, act; body, group
	mania	intense craving, loss of reason		
	phile	love, loving		
	phob	fear of		

DIRECTIONS: In Column A, identify the elements in each word by circling roots and underlining prefixes and suffixes. Then match each word with its correct meaning from Column B.

COLUMN A		COLUMN B
1. bibliophobia	____	a. list of books
2. biblioklept	____	b. excessive preoccupation with books
3. bibliology	____	c. lover of books
4. bibliography	____	d. dread or hatred of books
5. bibliophile	____	e. history and science of books as physical objects
6. bibliomania	____	f. one who steals books
7. kleptomania	____	g. obsession with one object or idea
8. graphomania	____	h. persistent craving to steal
9. monomania	____	i. obsessive desire to write

DIRECTIONS: Choose the best word from Column A for each sentence. Use each word only once.

1. A person who suffers from _____ would most likely not enjoy reading.

2. The librarian caught the _____ hiding several books under his jacket.

3. The piles of books and magazines in every corner attested to his _____.

4. The young girl's _____ caused her to write on walls, books, and her hands.

5. A true _____ appreciates not only the reading of books but also their design.

6. The family recognized their uncle's _____ when he started taking small items.

7. Experts in _____ can tell how books have evolved.

8. The writer's focus on spiders became a form of _____.

9. Titles of other works can be found in the _____ at the end of the book.

FOCUS: anthrop/anthropo

PREFIX	ROOT		SUFFIX	
	anthrop/	mankind, man	**-ic**	like, related to
	anthropo*		**-logy**	study of, science
	meter	measure	**-oid**	resembling
	nom	name, law, custom, order	**-y**	state of, quality, act; body, group
	path	feeling, disease		
	phil	love, loving		

DIRECTIONS: In Column A, identify the elements in each word by circling roots and underlining prefixes and suffixes. Then match each word with its correct meaning from Column B.

COLUMN A

1. (anthrop)oid _____
2. philanthropy _____
3. anthropology _____
4. anthropometer _____
5. anthroponomy _____
6. anthropopathic _____

COLUMN B

a. study of mankind
b. device used to measure the proportions of the human body
c. resembling man
d. love of mankind
e. relating human feelings to something not human
f. natural laws of human development as they relate to the environment

DIRECTIONS: Choose the best word from Column A for each sentence. Use each word only once.

1. The renowned humanitarian showed his _____ in several ways.

2. They decided the statue should be more _____ than abstract.

3. _____ includes the study of cave men.

4. An _____ has been used in studying the physical evolution of human beings.

5. Some religions have given their gods _____ qualities.

6. Current research in _____ focuses on global warming's potential effects for humans.

FOCUS: log/logo

PREFIX		ROOT		SUFFIX	
eu-	good, well	**gram**	write, written	**-ic**	like, related to
mono-	one	**log/**	word, reason	**-ism**	act, state, condition
		logo		**-y**	state of, quality, act; body, group
		mania	intense craving, loss of reason		
		neo*	new, recent		

DIRECTIONS: In Column A, identify the elements in each word by circling roots and underlining prefixes and suffixes. Then match each word with its correct meaning from Column B.

COLUMN A

1. (log)ic _____
2. e u l o g y _____
3. l o g o g r a m _____
4. l o g o m a n i a _____
5. m o n o l o g _____
6. n e o l o g i s m _____

COLUMN B

a. abnormal talkativeness
b. long speech given by one person
c. new word or phrase
d. related to theory of reasoning (Philosophy)
e. speech in praise of someone
f. symbol used to represent an entire word

DIRECTIONS: Choose the best word from Column A for each sentence. Use each word only once.

1. The talk show host's _____ lasted more than fifteen minutes.

2. The professor asked the student to explain the _____ behind his theory.

3. Her _____ seemed to occur whenever she was nervous.

4. The advertising agent tried to create a _____ to draw attention to the new product.

5. The mayor gave the _____ at the senator's funeral.

6. The $ is a _____ used to represent the word *dollar*.

FOCUS: ideo

PREFIX	ROOT		SUFFIX	
	crac	government, rule	**-ia**	condition
	gen	cause, birth, race, produce	**-logy**	study of, science
	gram	write, written	**-y**	state of, quality, act, body, group
	ideo*	idea		
	phob	fear of		
	phone	sound		

DIRECTIONS: In Column A, identify the elements in each word by circling roots and underlining prefixes and suffixes. Then match each word with its correct meaning from Column B.

COLUMN A

1. (ideo)(crac)y _____
2. ideogeny _____
3. ideogram _____
4. ideophobia _____
5. ideology _____
6. ideophone _____

COLUMN B

a. origin of ideas (Philosophy)
b. sound or pattern of sounds used to represent a concept
c. government based on an all-embracing idea or theory
d. system of interrelated social beliefs and values
e. graphic symbol used to represent a concept or word
f. fear or distrust of ideas

DIRECTIONS: Choose the best word from Column A for each sentence. Use each word only once.

1. Books are a focus of attack for those with _____.

2. Her theory of concept formation appears to be at odds with Aristotelian _____.

3. A picture of a light bulb is an _____ meaning idea or solution.

4. The student studied socialism's _____ and its effects on Eastern Europe.

5. The Russian government in the 1950s was a form of totalitarian _____.

6. Many African dialects use a combination of _____(s) and words.

FOCUS: peri-

PREFIX	ROOT		SUFFIX	
peri- around, surrounding	**cardi** heart **heli** sun **meter** measure **opt** eye, vision **scope** look at, view, examine		**-al** like, related to; an action or process **-ic** like, related to **-on** quality, state	

DIRECTIONS: In Column A, identify the elements in each word by circling roots and underlining prefixes and suffixes. Then match each word with its correct meaning from Column B.

COLUMN A

1. peri(meter) ____
2. pericardial ____
3. periscope ____
4. perihelion ____
5. perioptic ____

COLUMN B

a. point closest to the sun in a planet's orbit (Astronomy)
b. situated about or surrounding the eyeball (Medical)
c. instrument for viewing the surrounding area, especially objects not in the direct line of sight
d. situated around the heart (Biology)
e. circumference or distance around a figure

DIRECTIONS: Choose the best word from Column A for each sentence. Use each word only once.

1. The _____ fluid around one of our vital organs protects it from friction.

2. He needed to determine the _____ of the lot before building a fence.

3. Physicians discovered a _____ tumor was impairing his vision.

4. Astronomers have been able to pinpoint the _____ of Mars.

5. With the development of fiber optics, the _____ has become useful in medicine for locating tumors.

FOCUS: phon/phono

PREFIX		ROOT		SUFFIX	
sym-	with, together	**gen**	cause, birth, race, produce	**-ia**	condition
		homo*	same	**-ic**	like, related to
		path	feeling, disease	**-logy**	study of, science
		phob	fear of	**-y**	state of, quality, act; body, group
		phon/ phono	sound		
		poly*	many		
		tele*	from afar		

DIRECTIONS: In Column A, identify the elements in each word by circling roots and underlining prefixes and suffixes. Then match each word with its correct meaning from Column B.

COLUMN A		COLUMN B
1. (phon)ic _____		a. speech disorder
2. phonogenic _____		b. having many sounds (Music)
3. phonology _____		c. fear of sound or speaking
4. phonopathy _____		d. related to transmission of sound from a distance
5. phonophobia _____		e. related to the combining or harmony of sounds
6. homophonic _____		f. suitable for producing sound
7. polyphonic _____		g. related to sound
8. telephonic _____		h. study of speech sounds
9. symphonic _____		i. having the same sound

DIRECTIONS: Underline the best word for each sentence. Use each word only once.

1. His (phonology, phonopathy) caused him to stutter uncontrollably.

2 The quartet performed a complex (telephonic, symphonic) musical piece.

3. The two words were (homophonic, polyphonic) but had different meanings.

4. Early cavemen learned that even rocks and sticks were (phonic, phonogenic).

5. Reading teachers utilize (phonology, phonopathy) to develop word attack skills.

6. In a (polyphonic, homophonic) composition, each voice has its own distinct melody.

7. Matching letters with their sounds is a (phonogenic, phonic) approach to reading.

8. The (polyphonic, telephonic) device enabled him to communicate worldwide.

9. The woman's (phonopathy, phonophobia) made her avoid busy locations like the mall.

FOCUS: geo

PREFIX	ROOT		SUFFIX	
	centr	center	**-al**	like, related to; an action or process
	chron	time		
	gen	cause, birth, race, produce	**-er**	one who, that which
			-ic	like, related to
	geo	earth, ground	**-logy**	study of, science
	graph	write, written	**-ous**	having the quality of
	therm	heat	**-y**	state of, quality, act; body, group

DIRECTIONS: In Column A, identify the elements in each word by circling roots and underlining prefixes and suffixes. Then match each word with its correct meaning from Column B.

COLUMN A

1. (geo)(chron)y _____
2. geology _____
3. geocentric _____
4. geothermal _____
5. geogenous _____
6. geographer _____

COLUMN B

a. one who writes about the earth's features

b. growing on or in the ground

c. related to the heat of the earth's interior

d. related to the earth's center; earth-centered

e. system of time divisions used in the study of the earth

f. study of the earth's structure

DIRECTIONS: Underline the best word for each sentence. Use each word only once.

1. As a (geographer, geochrony), one must be extremely knowledgeable in all aspects of the earth's composition.

2. Epochs, periods, and eras are terms primarily related to (geochrony, geology).

3. Geysers are a source of (geogenous, geothermal) energy.

4. Most plants that are (geocentric, geogenous) have root systems.

5. Early Greek astronomers developed a (geogenous, geocentric) model of the solar system.

6. Volcanoes and glaciers are part of the (geochrony, geology) of the earth.

FOCUS: meso

PREFIX	ROOT		SUFFIX	
	crac	government, rule	**-ic**	like, related to
	derm	skin	**-y**	state of, quality, act; body, group
	meso*	middle		
	phil	love, loving		
	somat	body		
	therm	heat		

DIRECTIONS: In Column A, identify the elements in each word by circling roots and underlining prefixes and suffixes. Then match each word with its correct meaning from Column B.

COLUMN A

1. (meso)(derm)ic ____
2. m e s o c r a c y ____
3. m e s o t h e r m ____
4. m e s o p h i l i c ____
5. m e s o s o m a t i c ____

COLUMN B

a. related to the middle region of the body of various invertebrates (Zoology)

b. plant that requires a moderate degree of heat (Botany)

c. thriving in a moderate environment (Biology)

d. related to the middle layer of skin (Biology)

e. government by the middle classes

DIRECTIONS: Underline the best word for each sentence. Use each word only once.

1. A (mesocracy, mesotherm) is similar in nature to a democracy.

2. The proper formation of the (mesophilic, mesodermic) layer is crucial in the final development of all connective tissue.

3. The (mesosomatic, mesophilic) portion of a spider's body is often difficult to locate.

4. A (mesotherm, mesocracy) would not survive in the regions where it snows.

5. Scientists study the conditions necessary to cultivate (mesophilic, mesosomatic) bacteria.

FOCUS: path/patho, somat/somato

PREFIX		ROOT		SUFFIX	
a-	away, from; not, without	**gen**	cause, birth, race, produce	**-ic**	like, related to
anti-	against, opposite	**metr**	measure	**-logy**	study of, science
sym-	with, together	**path/ patho**	feeling, disease	**-y**	state of, quality, act; body, group
		psycho	mind, spirit		
		somat/ somato	body		

DIRECTIONS: In Column A, identify the elements in each word by circling roots and underlining prefixes and suffixes. Then match each word with its correct meaning from Column B.

COLUMN A

1. (psycho)(somat)<u>ic</u> ____
2. somatogenic ____
3. somatology ____
4. somatometry ____
5. antipathy ____
6. apathy ____
7. sympathy ____
8. pathology ____
9. psychopathology ____

COLUMN B

a. study of disease
b. supporting another's viewpoint; ability to share another's feelings
c. related to the effect of the mind on the body (Medical)
d. study of mental illness
e. feeling of dislike or opposition toward something
f. originating in the cells of the body (Medical)
g. lack of feeling
h. study of human physical characteristics (Anthropology)
i. related to body measurement (Anthropology)

DIRECTIONS: Underline the best word for each sentence. Use each word only once.

1. (Somatology, Somatometry) deals with changes in body proportions in humans.

2. The (apathy, sympathy) coming from his listeners encouraged the speaker to continue.

3. The boy's paralysis was (somatogenic, psychosomatic) and could be overcome with psychotherapy.

4. My mother felt a strong (antipathy, somatology) towards any kind of insect.

5. Researchers in (somatometry, psychopathology) investigate the effects of schizophrenia.

6. The source of the bacterial infection was determined to be (psychosomatic, somatogenic).

7. His continued (apathy, sympathy) made it difficult to generate enthusiasm.

8. The sample was sent to the (psychopathology, pathology) lab to test for cancer.

9. (Somatology, Pathology) compares Neanderthal man with Cro-Magnon.

FOCUS: dia

PREFIX		ROOT		SUFFIX	
dia-	through, across	**chron**	time	**-ic**	like, related to
		derm	skin	**-y**	state of, quality, act; body, group
		log	word, reason		
		meter	measure		
		therm	heat		

DIRECTIONS: In Column A, identify the elements in each word by circling roots and underlining prefixes and suffixes. Then match each word with its correct meaning from Column B.

COLUMN A

1. dia(log) _____

2. diameter _____

3. diathermy _____

4. diachronic _____

5. diadermic _____

COLUMN B

a. generation of heat in body tissue by electric current (Medical)

b. acting through the skin

c. considering phenomena, such as languages, as they change over time

d. conversation between two or more persons

e. line passing through the center of a figure

DIRECTIONS: Underline the best word for each sentence. Use each word only once.

1. The (diachronic, diadermic) ointment alleviated her pain.

2. Their (dialog, diathermy) had become a rather heated argument.

3. The surgeon relied on (dialog, diathermy) to desensitize the tissue during the operation.

4. The linguist wrote a (diadermic, diachronic) description of the use of Latin roots in the English language.

5. The (diameter, diathermy) of the opening was six inches.

FOCUS: ant-/anti-

PREFIX		ROOT		SUFFIX	
ant-/ **anti-**	against, opposite	**bio**	life	**-on**	quality, state
sym-	with, together	**heli**	sun	**-sis**	action, process
		log	word, reason	**-y**	state of, quality, act; body, group
		metr	measure		
		nom	name, law, custom, order		
		onym	name, word		
		path	feeling, disease		
		phon	sound		

DIRECTIONS: In Column A, identify the elements in each word by circling roots and underlining prefixes and suffixes. Then match each word with its correct meaning from Column B.

COLUMN A

1. anti<u>log</u>y _____
2. antiphony _____
3. antinomy _____
4. anthelion _____
5. antonym _____
6. antipathy _____
7. antibiosis _____
8. antisymmetry _____

COLUMN B

a. bright spot occurring opposite the sun

b. association between organisms which is injurious to one of them

c. feeling of dislike or opposition towards something

d. opposition of sounds between two groups

e. contradiction in terms or ideas

f. opposing, irregular properties

g. opposition of one law to another

h. word that is opposite in meaning

DIRECTIONS: Underline the best word for each sentence. Use each word only once.

1. The congregation and the choir created an (antinomy, antiphony).

2. Astronomers have not been able to account for the recent appearance of an (anthelion, antonym).

3. Some parasites create an (anthelion, antibiosis) which results in the host organism's death.

4. The teacher instructed us to find an (antinomy, antonym) for each of our spelling words.

5. My mother had a strong (antipathy, antiphony) for spicy foods.

6. The chaos within their country was due to the (antinomy, antibiosis) in their legal system.

7. There seemed to be an (antinomy, antilogy) in the reasoning he gave for his actions.

8. The (antinomy, antisymmetry) of the house's proportions made it more interesting to look at.

FOCUS: metr/metro

PREFIX		ROOT		SUFFIX	
sym-	with, together	**bio**	life	**-ic**	like, related to
		metr/	measure	**-logy**	study of, science
		metro		**-y**	state of, quality, act; body, group
		nome	name, law, custom, order		
		opto	eye, vision		
		psycho	mind, spirit		
		somato	body		

DIRECTIONS: In Column A, identify the elements in each word by circling roots and underlining prefixes and suffixes. Then match each word with its correct meaning from Column B.

COLUMN A

1. (met)ic   _____
2. symmetric   _____
3. biometry   _____
4. metrology   _____
5. optometry   _____
6. psychometric   _____
7. somatometry   _____
8. metronome   _____

COLUMN B

a. science of weights and measures

b. testing of eyes to measure vision

c. related to the measurement of mental data

d. related to body measurement (Anthropology)

e. device used to measure rhythm

f. having corresponding parts the same in size and form

g. statistical analysis of biological observations and phenomena

h. related to the system of meters

DIRECTIONS: Underline the best word for each sentence. Use each word only once.

1. The lovely floral arrangement was perfectly (metric, symmetric).

2. The patient required (optometry, somatometry) to determine the degree of his visual impairment.

3. The (metric, psychometric) examination enabled the counselor to assess the student's ability.

4. Advances in (biometry, somatometry) have increased our knowledge of how early man looked.

5. Experts in the field of (biometry, somatometry) utilize many factors in projecting life span.

6. His piano teacher used a (biometry, metronome) to help him keep the correct tempo.

7. Gemologists use (metrology, optometry) in determining the carat weight of gems.

8. They no longer measure distance in miles since they converted to the (metric, symmetric) system.

FOCUS: bronch/broncho

PREFIX	ROOT		SUFFIX	
	bronch/	throat, airways	**-ic**	like, related to
	broncho		**-itis**	inflammation
	gen	cause, birth, race, produce	**-y**	state of, quality, act; body, group
	gram	write, written		
	phon	sound		
	scope	look at, view, examine		

DIRECTIONS: In Column A, identify the elements in each word by circling roots and underlining prefixes and suffixes. Then match each word with its correct meaning from Column B.

COLUMN A

1. bronchogram ____
2. bronchitis ____
3. bronchophony ____
4. bronchogenic ____
5. bronchoscope ____

COLUMN B

a. originating from the air passages of the lungs (Medical)

b. thin tube which enables a doctor to see into the airways

c. an X-ray of the air passages

d. inflammation of the air passages

e. sound of the voice heard through the stethoscope over healthy lungs (Medical)

DIRECTIONS: Choose the best word from Column A for each sentence. Use each word only once.

1. The doctor diagnosed her patient as having chronic _____.

2. The patient's _____ showed damage from a previous infection.

3. Coughing and sneezing are _____ sources of infection.

4. After listening to the patient's _____, the doctor indicated the patient's airways were clear.

5. The physician inserted a _____ into the patient's throat to determine the extent of the damage.

FOCUS: cardi/cardio

PREFIX		ROOT		SUFFIX	
peri-	around, surrounding	**cardi/ cardio**	heart	**-ac**	related to, pertaining to
		graph	write, written	**-al**	like, related to; an action or process
		path	feeling, disease	**-logy**	study of, science
				-y	state of, quality, act; body, group

DIRECTIONS: In Column A, identify the elements in each word by circling roots and underlining prefixes and suffixes. Then match each word with its correct meaning from Column B.

COLUMN A

1. <u>peri</u>(card)<u>al</u> ____
2. cardiac ____
3. cardiology ____
4. cardiopathy ____
5. cardiograph ____

COLUMN B

a. instrument that graphically records the heart's movements
b. disease of the heart (Medical)
c. situated around the heart (Biology)
d. pertaining to the heart
e. study of the heart

DIRECTIONS: Write the best word from Column A for each sentence. Use each word only once.

1. A doctor can use a _____ to monitor the patient's heart during surgery.

2. The elderly man suffered from a _____ condition that limited his activity.

3. Surgeons found a tear in his _____ sac.

4. Medical students in the field of _____ may one day perform a transplant.

5. Researchers followed the development of 300 newborns diagnosed with congenital _____.

FOCUS: micro

PREFIX	ROOT		SUFFIX	
	bio	life	**-ic**	like, related to
	cosm	universe, harmony	**-logy**	study of, science
	graph	write, written		
	meter	measure		
	micro*	small		
	scop	look at, view, examine		

DIRECTIONS: In Column A, identify the elements in each word by circling roots and underlining prefixes and suffixes. Then match each word with its correct meaning from Column B.

COLUMN A

1. microbiology _____
2. microcosm _____
3. micrograph _____
4. micrometer _____
5. microscopic _____

COLUMN B

a. instrument for accurately measuring small distances
b. too small to be seen by the naked eye
c. the study of minute forms of life
d. small world; a miniature copy of a larger whole
e. picture or drawing of something seen through a microscope

DIRECTIONS: Choose the best word from Column A for each sentence. Use each word only once.

1. Viruses and bacteria are _____ forms of life.

2. A single drop of pond water is a _____ of its own.

3. To gauge the size of the screw threads, she used a _____.

4. The military uses researchers in the field of _____.

5. The textbook on marine biology included _____(s) of plankton.

FOCUS: arch

PREFIX		ROOT		SUFFIX	
an-	not, without	**arch**	first, chief, rule	**-y**	state of, quality, act; body, group
mon-	one	**gyn**	woman, female		
syn-	with, together				
tri-	three				

DIRECTIONS: In Column A, identify the elements in each word by circling roots and underlining prefixes and suffixes. Then match each word with its correct meaning from Column B.

COLUMN A   COLUMN B

1. an(arch)y _____   a. rule or government by three persons
2. triarchy _____   b. joint rule
3. monarchy _____   c. absence of rule
4. gynarchy _____   d. rule by one person
5. synarchy _____   e. rule by women

DIRECTIONS: Underline the best word for each sentence. Use each word only once.

1. Political unrest can lead to a state of (triarchy, anarchy) in a country.

2. The legendary tribe of Amazon women would have exemplified a (gynarchy, triarchy).

3. In medieval times, the king, prime minister, and archbishop formed a (triarchy, synarchy).

4. British colonists in Africa joined with the native ministers in a (monarchy, synarchy).

5. Britain was a (triarchy, monarchy) for several centuries.

FOCUS: crac

PREFIX	ROOT		SUFFIX	
	andro*	man, male	**-y**	state of, quality, act; body, group
	auto*	self		
	crac	government, rule		
	gyno	woman, female		
	ideo*	idea		
	meso*	middle		

DIRECTIONS: In Column A, identify the elements in each word by circling roots and underlining prefixes and suffixes. Then match each word with its correct meaning from Column B.

COLUMN A

1. androcracy _____
2. autocracy _____
3. gynocracy _____
4. ideocracy _____
5. mesocracy _____

COLUMN B

a. government by the middle classes
b. political and social rule by men
c. rule by one person with unlimited power
d. government by women
e. government based on an all-embracing idea or theory

DIRECTIONS: Choose the best word for each sentence from Column A. Use each word only once.

1. _____ is a form of government similar to that of the United States.

2. The small republic became an _____ when its government was overthrown by the corrupt general.

3. The principles of an _____ tend to be fanatical.

4. In ancient China, a form of _____ among wealthy families gave the mother significant control.

5. In many countries, _____ has kept women from having a voice in political decisions affecting them.

FOCUS: meter

PREFIX	ROOT		SUFFIX
peri- around, surrounding	bio	life	
	chrono	time	
	hydro*	water	
	meter	measure	
	micro*	small	
	phono	sound	
	thermo	heat	

DIRECTIONS: In Column A, identify the elements in each word by circling roots and underlining prefixes and suffixes. Then match each word with its correct meaning from Column B.

COLUMN A

1. biometer _____
2. chronometer _____
3. hydrometer _____
4. micrometer _____
5. perimeter _____
6. phonometer _____
7. thermometer _____

COLUMN B

a. instrument which measures heat

b. instrument for measuring the specific gravity of liquids

c. instrument which measures the intensity of sound

d. circumference or distance around a figure

e. instrument for accurately measuring small distances

f. device that measures carbon dioxide given off by living matter (Biology)

g. timekeeping device of great accuracy, especially used in measuring longitude

DIRECTIONS: Choose the best word for each sentence from Column A. Use each word only once.

1. The _____ registered an increase in temperature.

2. He used a _____ to determine which items would float.

3. The audio technician required a _____ to determine the correct volume for recording.

4. The contractor needed to know the exact _____ of the building.

5. The _____ calculated the exact time it took for the bullet to reach the target.

6. A _____ measures the output of organisms in chemically treated soils.

7. A _____ was attached to the microscope to determine the diameter of the cell.

FOCUS: gram

PREFIX		ROOT		SUFFIX
dia-	through, across	**cardio**	heart	
mono-	one	**gram**	write, written	
		logo	word, reason	
		phono	sound	
		tele*	from afar	

DIRECTIONS: In Column A, identify the elements in each word by circling roots and underlining prefixes and suffixes. Then match each word with its correct meaning from Column B.

COLUMN A

1. (phono)(gram) _____

2. monogram _____

3. telegram _____

4. cardiogram _____

5. diagram _____

6. logogram _____

COLUMN B

a. drawing or design showing the relationship between parts of a whole

b. symbol used to represent an entire word

c. letter or symbol that represents a sound

d. written message sent from a distance

e. one or more single letters (such as initials) used to represent a name

f. record of the heart's movements

DIRECTIONS: Choose the best word from Column A for each sentence. Use each word only once.

1. The vacationing couple sent greetings by _____.

2. The bride selected linens with a _____ of her new name.

3. The specialist waited for the results of the patient's _____ before making his diagnosis.

4. The student checked the _____ shown in the dictionary before pronouncing the word.

5. He assembled the bicycle by following the enclosed _____.

6. The company designed a _____ of its name for easier product recognition.

FOCUS: phob

PREFIX		ROOT		SUFFIX	
mono-	one	cardio	heart	-ia	condition
		gyno	woman, female		
		hydro*	water		
		klepto	to steal		
		neo*	new, recent		
		phob	fear of		
		xeno	foreign, strange		

DIRECTIONS: In Column A, identify the elements in each word by circling roots and underlining prefixes and suffixes. Then match each word with its correct meaning from Column B.

COLUMN A

1. cardiophobia _____
2. gynophobia _____
3. hydrophobia _____
4. kleptophobia _____
5. monophobia _____
6. neophobia _____
7. xenophobia _____

COLUMN B

a. fear of water
b. abnormal fear of being alone
c. abnormal fear of heart disease
d. fear of strangers
e. fear of stealing (or being stolen from)
f. fear of change or new things
g. fear of women

DIRECTIONS: Underline the best word for each sentence. Use each word only once.

1. The man's (gynophobia, monophobia) made him a confirmed bachelor.

2. People with (hydrophobia, xenophobia) are reluctant to leave home.

3. The legislative council's (kleptophobia, neophobia) was responsible for the stagnating economy.

4. Being in a crowd helped to ease her (monophobia, hydrophobia).

5. Someone with (hydrophobia, neophobia) might be afraid to go sailing.

6. Because of his (monophobia, cardiophobia), he refused to exert himself in any way.

7. Her (xenophobia, kleptophobia) caused her to watch her possessions carefully.

FOCUS: phil/phile/philo

PREFIX	ROOT		SUFFIX	
	anthrop	mankind, man	**-y**	state of, quality, act; body, group
	biblio	book		
	gyn	woman, female		
	log	word, reason		
	phil/ phile/ philo	love, loving		
	phono	sound		
	xeno	foreign, strange		

DIRECTIONS: In Column A, identify the elements in each word by circling roots and underlining prefixes and suffixes. Then match each word with its correct meaning from Column B.

COLUMN A

1. (phil)anthropy _____
2. bibliophile _____
3. philogyny _____
4. xenophile _____
5. philology _____
6. phonophile _____

COLUMN B

a. the love of learning and literature (literally, a fondness for words)

b. lover of foreign things

c. lover and collector of phonograph records

d. lover of books

e. fondness for women

f. love of mankind

DIRECTIONS: Choose the best word from Column A for each sentence. Use each word only once.

1. The devoted _____ travelled worldwide to collect new items.

2. The president's generosity towards those in need was a sign of his _____ .

3. His _____ did not extend to a support of women's rights.

4. Her collection of literary masterpieces was an indication that she was a _____.

5. The _____ owned a collection of works by all the great composers.

6. An expert in _____ would be very familiar with the classics.

FOCUS: hypo-

PREFIX	ROOT		SUFFIX	
hypo- under, below	**chrom**	color	**-ia**	condition
	derm	skin	**-ic**	like, related to
	ge	earth, ground		
	gen	cause, birth, race, produce	**-ous**	having the quality of
	mania	intense craving, loss of reasoning		
	therm	heat		

DIRECTIONS: In Column A, identify the elements in each word by circling roots and underlining prefixes and suffixes. Then match each word with its correct meaning from Column B.

COLUMN A

1. hypochromia _____
2. hypodermic _____
3. hypothermia _____
4. hypomania _____
5. hypogeous _____
6. hypogenous _____

COLUMN B

a. growing on the underside (Botany)
b. happening underground (Geology)
c. lack of color
d. under the skin
e. condition of reduced temperature
f. mild form of psychosis indicated by an elevated mood (Psychology)

DIRECTIONS: Underline the best word for each sentence. Use each word only once.

1. By the time the stranded mountain climbers were rescued, they were suffering from (hypochromia, hypothermia).

2. Most ferns have (hypogeous, hypogenous) spores on their fronds.

3. The (hypomania, hypochromia) of the plant's leaves was an indication that it needed to be fertilized.

4. A volcanic eruption can be the result of (hypogeous, hypodermic) forces.

5. The technician used a (hypogenous, hypodermic) needle to take a blood sample.

6. One suffering from (hypomania, hypochromia) might exhibit increased activity or a state of elation.

FOCUS: cycl/cycle/cyclo, klept/klepto

PREFIX		ROOT		SUFFIX	
bi-	two	**biblio**	book	**-ia**	condition
tri-	three	**cycl/ cycle/ cyclo**	circle	**-ic**	like, related to
		gen	cause, birth, race, produce		
		klept/ klepto	to steal		
		mania	intense craving, loss of reason		
		meter	measure		
		phob	fear of		

DIRECTIONS: In Column A, identify the elements in each word by circling roots and underlining prefixes and suffixes. Then match each word with its correct meaning from Column B.

COLUMN A

1. biblioklept   ____
2. kleptomania   ____
3. kleptophobia   ____
4. bicycle   ____
5. cyclometer   ____
6. cyclic   ____
7. tricycle   ____
8. cyclogenic   ____

COLUMN B

a. device that measures number of rotations of a wheel to indicate distance travelled
b. vehicle with three wheels
c. relating to life cycles
d. fear of stealing (or being stolen from)
e. occurring or repeating in cycles
f. one who steals books
g. vehicle with two wheels
h. persistent craving to steal

DIRECTIONS: Choose the best word from Column A for each sentence. Use each word only once.

1. The metamorphosis from caterpillar to butterfly is a form of _____ development.

2. The padlocked doors and windows attested to her _____.

3. Several bookstores in the area have lost merchandise to the same _____.

4. The changing of the seasons is a _____ phenomenon.

5. Taking small items from other students' desks was an early sign of her _____.

6. It is easier for a young child to learn to ride a _____.

7. A serious cyclist will install a _____ on his _____ to monitor his trips.

FOCUS: macro

PREFIX	ROOT		SUFFIX	
	bio	life	**-ic**	like, related to
	cosm	universe, harmony	**-sis**	action, process
	graph	write, written		
	macro*	large, great		
	mania	intense craving, loss of reason		
	scop	look at, view, examine		

DIRECTIONS: In Column A, identify the elements in each word by circling roots and underlining prefixes and suffixes. Then match each word with its correct meaning from Column B.

COLUMN A

1. (macr(bio)sis) ____
2. macrocosm ____
3. macrograph ____
4. macromania ____
5. macroscopic ____

COLUMN B

a. an image that is equal to or larger than the object
b. visible to the naked eye
c. longevity
d. big world or universe
e. delusion that things are larger than they really are

DIRECTIONS: Underline the best word for each sentence. Use each word only once.

1. Scientists continue to search ways to achieve _____.

2. The company placed a _____ of the product inside the magazine.

3. Consumers would prefer to have _____ print on contracts.

4. Her fear of spiders was intensified by her _____ .

5. Our planet is but a speck in the _____.

FOCUS: sym-/syn-

PREFIX		ROOT		SUFFIX	
anti-	against, opposite	**arch**	first, chief, rule	**-ic**	like, related to
sym-/	with, together	**bio**	life	**-ous**	having the quality of
syn-		**chron**	time	**-sis**	action, process
		metr	measure	**-y**	state of, quality, act; body, group
		onym	name, word		
		opt	eye, vision		
		path	feeling, disease		
		phon	sound		

DIRECTIONS: In Column A, identify the elements in each word by circling roots and underlining prefixes and suffixes. Then match each word with its correct meaning from Column B.

COLUMN A

1. <u>anti</u>sym(metr)<u>ic</u> ____

2. symbiosis ____

3. sympathy ____

4. symphonic ____

5. synarchy ____

6. synchronous ____

7. synonymous ____

8. synoptic ____

COLUMN B

a. supporting another's viewpoint, ability to share another's feelings

b. occurring at the same time

c. taking a general view of the whole subject

d. having a similar meaning (Linguistics)

e. having opposite and irregular properties

f. living together of two dissimilar organisms in a mutually beneficial relationship (Biology)

g. joint rule

h. related to the combining or harmony of sounds

DIRECTIONS: Underline the best word for each sentence. Use each word only once.

1. The (sympathy, symbiosis) between pilot fish and sharks is well known.

2. Several instruments were brought together for a (synonymous, symphonic) performance.

3. The (antisymmetric, symphonic) arrangement of the parts made it difficult to put together.

4. We had to time everything carefully to ensure the events would be (synonymous, synchronous).

5. The (synonymous, antisymmetric) words were interchangeable in the sentence.

6. At one time, Britain thrived under a (symbiosis, synarchy) of church and state.

7. His (symphonic, synoptic) report wasn't much more than a summary.

8. The (sympathy, synarchy) of friends and family was a comfort to the grieving wife.

FOCUS: helio

PREFIX	ROOT		SUFFIX	
	centr	center	**-ic**	like, related to
	graph	write, written	**-sis**	action, process
	helio	sun		
	meter	measure		
	phile	love, loving		
	scope	look at, view, examine		

DIRECTIONS: In Column A, identify the elements in each word by circling roots and underlining prefixes and suffixes. Then match each word with its correct meaning from Column B.

COLUMN A

1. (helio)(meter) ____
2. helioscope ____
3. heliocentric ____
4. heliograph ____
5. heliophile ____

COLUMN B

a. centered on the sun

b. one attracted to sunlight

c. device originally designed to measure the sun's diameter and the angles between stars

d. device for viewing the sun

e. device for telegraphing by means of the sun's rays

DIRECTIONS: Choose the best word from Column A for each sentence. Use each word only once.

1. They watched the solar eclipse through a _____ .

2. Skin cancer is a definite risk for the _____.

3. Photographic methods have made the _____ obsolete for measuring celestial angles.

4. The _____ probably did not function well when the sky was overcast.

5. The planets in our solar system share a _____ orbit.

FOCUS: scop/scope

PREFIX	ROOT		SUFFIX
peri- around, surrounding	**cardio**	heart	**-ic** like, related to
	hydro*	water	
	macro*	large, great	
	micro*	small	
	phone	sound	
	scop/	look at, view, examine	
	scope		
	tele*	from afar	

DIRECTIONS: In Column A, identify the elements in each word by circling roots and underlining prefixes and suffixes. Then match each word with its correct meaning from Column B.

COLUMN A

1. (cardio)(scope) ____
2. hydroscope ____
3. telescope ____
4. microscopic ____
5. periscope ____
6. phonoscope ____
7. macroscopic ____

COLUMN B

a. instrument for viewing surrounding area, especially objects not in the direct line of sight

b. too small to be seen by the naked eye

c. instrument for viewing the interior of the heart

d. instrument that makes distant objects appear nearer and larger

e. instrument which represents sound vibrations in a visible form

f. visible to the naked eye

g. device for viewing objects below the surface of water

DIRECTIONS: Choose the best word from Column A for each sentence. Use each word only once.

1. The _____ allowed the marine biologist to explore life at greater depths.

2. Submarines utilized the _____ for locating vehicles on the surface.

3. A _____ is an invaluable tool for surgeons performing open heart surgery.

4. Astronomers are able to view constellations that are light-years away using the latest _____.

5. A closer look revealed some _____ residue on his skin.

6. Bacteriologists are amazed at the diversity in the _____ world they study.

7. The tonal quality of the harp's strings was tested using a _____.

FOCUS: poly

PREFIX	ROOT		SUFFIX	
	arch	first, chief, rule	**-ic**	like, related to
	centr	center	**-ism**	act, state, condition
	chrome	color	**-ous**	having the quality of
	gam	united, joined	**-y**	state of, quality, act; body, group
	gen	cause, birth, race, produce		
	onym	name, word		
	phon	sound		
	poly*	many		
	the	god		

DIRECTIONS: In Column A, identify the elements in each word by circling roots and underlining prefixes and suffixes. Then match each word with its correct meaning from Column B.

COLUMN A

1. polyphonic _____
2. polychrome _____
3. polytheism _____
4. polyonymous _____
5. polyarchy _____
6. polygenic _____
7. polycentric _____
8. polygamy _____

COLUMN B

a. belief in many gods
b. coming from multiple genes (Biology)
c. rule by many
d. having more than one spouse at the same time
e. many-colored
f. having many names
g. having many sounds (Music)
h. having more than one center, having multiple centers of control (Biology, Political Science)

DIRECTIONS: Choose the best word from Column A for each sentence. Use each word only once.

1. Many authors are _____ and write under several different pen names.

2. Stories of Zeus and Athena are evidence that the ancient Greeks practiced _____.

3. The bright and beautiful quilt had a _____ background.

4. Your local city council is a form of _____.

5. _____ choral compositions require numerous vocal parts.

6. Animals displaying _____ traits are selectively bred to get the desired result.

7. The practice of _____ was common for men in many Arab countries.

8. City planners debated the merits of _____ urban growth.

FOCUS: gyn/gyno

PREFIX	ROOT		SUFFIX	
mono- one	**andro**	man, male	**-ia**	condition
	crac	government, rule	**-ous**	having the quality of
	gyn/	woman, female	**-y**	state of, quality, act; body, group
	gyno			
	miso*	to hate		
	phob	fear of		

DIRECTIONS: In Column A, identify the elements in each word by circling roots and underlining prefixes and suffixes. Then match each word with its correct meaning from Column B.

COLUMN A

1. androgynous ____
2. gynocracy ____
3. gynophobia ____
4. misogyny ____
5. monogynous ____

COLUMN B

a. hatred of women
b. fear of women
c. having only one wife at a time
d. government by women
e. having both male and female characteristics

DIRECTIONS: Underline the best word to complete each sentence. Use each word only once.

1. Whoever designed stiletto heels must have been influenced by (gynophobia, misogyny).

2. (Monogynous, Androgynous) animals, such as the earthworm, produce both sperm and eggs.

3. The doctor believed that Stan's (gynarchy, gynophobia) was a product of his abusive childhood.

4. It is the common practice in most Western countries for married men to be (monogynous, androgynous).

5. Historical examples of (misogyny, gynocracy) are prevalent in monarchies.

FOCUS: tele

PREFIX	ROOT		SUFFIX	
	gra/ **gram**	write, written	**-y**	state of, quality, act; body, group
	metr	measure		
	path	feeling, disease		
	phone	sound		
	scope	look at, view, examine		
	tele*	from afar		
	thermo	heat		

DIRECTIONS: In Column A, identify the elements in each word by circling roots and underlining prefixes and suffixes. Then match each word with its correct meaning from Column B.

COLUMN A

1. telepathy ____
2. telescope ____
3. telemetry ____
4. telephone ____
5. telegram ____
6. telethermometry ____
7. telegraphone ____

COLUMN B

a. device that transmits sound from a distance

b. communication between minds

c. written message sent from a distance

d. early device for recording sound

e. measurement of the distance of an object from an observer

f. process for making remote temperature measurements

g. instrument that makes distant objects appear nearer and larger

DIRECTIONS: Choose the best word from Column A for each sentence. Use each word only once.

1. Astronomers use a more powerful _____ to study distant universes.

2. In 1898, Oberlin Smith patented the _____, the first magnetic recording device.

3. He received a _____ from friends while touring Europe.

4. A rifle's scope is used to determine the _____ between the target and hunter.

5. The new _____ used a system of satellite cells to transmit her voice.

6. Scientists utilize _____ to help determine the climate of planets like Mars.

7. The psychic attempted to locate the missing child through _____.

FOCUS: neo

PREFIX	ROOT		SUFFIX	
	anthrop	mankind, man	**-esis**	action, process
	cosm	universe, harmony	**-ia**	condition
	crac	government, rule	**-ic**	like, related to
	gen	cause, birth, race, produce	**-ism**	act, state, condition
	log	word, reason	**-y**	state of, quality, act; body, group
	neo*	new, recent		
	phob	fear of		

DIRECTIONS: In Column A, identify the elements in each word by circling roots and underlining prefixes and suffixes. Then match each word with its correct meaning from Column B.

COLUMN A

1. neologism _____
2. neocosmic _____
3. neophobia _____
4. neogenesis _____
5. neocracy _____
6. neoanthropic _____

COLUMN B

a. belonging to the same species as recent man (Anthropology)
b. government by those new to government
c. new formation (as of tissue) (Biology)
d. fear of change or new things
e. new word or phrase
f. related to the universe in its present state

DIRECTIONS: Choose the best word from Column A for each sentence. Use each word only once.

1. His acute _____ made it difficult for him to accept change.

2. Often, a _____ is generated from teenage slang.

3. A starfish is capable of _____ when it loses an arm.

4. Cro-Magnon, unlike the Neanderthal, is considered to be _____.

5. The small island formed a _____ following its declaration of independence.

6. Astronomers involved in _____ research rely on data from space stations.

FOCUS: mon-/mono-

PREFIX	ROOT		SUFFIX	
mon-/ one **mono-**	**arch**	first, chief, rule	**-ia**	condition
	centr	center	**-ic**	like, related to
	chrome	color	**-ism**	act, state, condition
	gen	cause, birth, race, produce	**-y**	state of, quality, act; body, group
	phob	fear of		
	phon	sound		
	the	god		

DIRECTIONS: In Column A, identify the elements in each word by circling roots and underlining prefixes and suffixes. Then match each word with its correct meaning from Column B.

COLUMN A   **COLUMN B**

1. <u>mono</u>(phob)<u>ia</u> ____   a. having a single or common origin

2. monocentric ____   b. made of shades of a single color

3. monogenic ____   c. having one sound

4. monophonic ____   d. belief in one god

5. monarchy ____   e. having a single center

6. monotheism ____   f. abnormal fear of being alone

7. monochrome ____   g. rule by one person

DIRECTIONS: Choose the best word from Column A for each sentence. Use each word only once.

1. A stereophonic recording produces a better sound than the old _____ ones.

2. Christianity is a religion based on _____.

3. The American colonists fought against rule by the British _____.

4. Igneous rocks near a volcanic vent were determined to be _____.

5. He found an old _____ etching of the building.

6. Her mother's increasing _____ required that they place her in a full-time care facility.

7. The fabric had a _____ floral design with multicolored petals.

FOCUS: gen/geno

PREFIX	ROOT		SUFFIX	
exo- outside	**bio**	life	**-ic**	like, related to
	gen/	cause, birth, race, produce	**-cide**	kill
	geno		**-ous**	having the quality of
	patho	feeling, disease	**-esis**	action, process
	psycho	mind, spirit		

DIRECTIONS: In Column A, identify the elements in each word by circling roots and underlining prefixes and suffixes. Then match each word with its correct meaning from Column B.

COLUMN A

1. (path)(gen)ic ____
2. biogenic ____
3. exogenous ____
4. genesis ____
5. genocide ____
6. psychogenic ____

COLUMN B

a. caused by a factor or agent outside the organism (Medical)
b. killing of a race
c. originating in the mind
d. causing disease
e. beginning or birth of something
f. produced by the action of living organisms (Geology)

DIRECTIONS: Underline the best word to complete each sentence. Use each word only once.

1. When hatred and war exist, there is always the danger of (genesis, genocide).

2. Asbestosis is a/an (psychogenic, exogenous) disease caused by environmental exposure.

3. Food poisoning is often the result of (psychogenic, pathogenic) bacteria.

4. The theory had its (genocide, genesis) several years earlier in a small laboratory.

5. The coral reefs off Australia are examples of (exogenous, biogenic) reef formation.

6. His (psychogenic, biogenic) seizures were directly related to his increasing stress.

FOCUS: bi-, dermat/dermato

PREFIX	ROOT		SUFFIX	
bi- two	**centr**	center	**-ic**	like, related to
	chrome	color	**-itis**	inflammation
	cycle	circle	**-logy**	study of, science
	dermat/ dermato	skin	**-osis**	condition
	graph	write, written		
	pod/ podo	foot		

DIRECTIONS: In Column A, identify the elements in each word by circling roots and underlining prefixes and suffixes. Then match each word with its correct meaning from Column B.

COLUMN A

1. bicentric _____
2. bichrome _____
3. bicycle _____
4. bipod _____
5. dermatitis _____
6. dermatograph _____
7. dermatology _____
8. dermatosis _____
9. pododermatitis _____

COLUMN B

a. study of the skin

b. inflammation of the skin tissue of the foot

c. disease of the skin

d. related to a classification of plant or animal with two centers of origin (Biology)

e. instrument for producing markings on skin

f. vehicle with two wheels

g. having two colors

h. inflammation of the skin

i. a two-legged support

DIRECTIONS: Underline the best word to complete each sentence. Use each word only once.

1. The surgeon used a (pododermatitis, dermatograph) to outline the organs for surgery.

2. Philistine pottery was (bicentric, bichrome) and usually painted in red and black.

3. His skin rash advanced from an inflammation to a serious (dermatosis, dermatitis).

4. Evidence indicated the lichen was (dermatosis, bicentric).

5. The marksman used a (bicycle, bipod) to level his rifle.

6. Skin cancer is currently a significant topic in (dermatology, pododermatitis).

7. They travelled by (bichrome, bicycle) throughout Europe.

8. The angry red rash on her arms indicated a case of (dermatitis, dermatograph).

9. He developed (bipod, pododermatitis) from the tight shoes.

PREFIX	ROOT		SUFFIX	
a- away, from; not, without	**acro**	height, top	**-ia**	condition
	agro	field	**-ology**	study of, science
	entom	insect	**-ous**	having the quality of
	hydro*	water		
	morph	form	**-y**	state of, quality, act; body, group
	nom	name, law, custom, order		
	phob	fear of		
	therap	treatment		

DIRECTIONS: In Column A, identify the elements in each word by circling roots and underlining prefixes and suffixes. Then match each word with its correct meaning from Column B.

COLUMN A

1. acrophobia _____
2. agronomy _____
3. amorphous _____
4. entomology _____
5. hydrotherapy _____

COLUMN B

a. without definite form, shapeless

b. management of farm land

c. branch of zoology that deals with insects

d. abnormal fear of high places

e. treatment of disease or injury by the use of baths, etc.

DIRECTIONS: Write a complete sentence for each word in Column A. Use each word only once.

1. _____

_____

2. _____

_____

3. _____

_____

4. _____

_____

5. _____

_____

PREFIX		ROOT		SUFFIX	
amphi-	both, around	**bi**	life	**-al**	like, related to; an action or process
epi-	on, outside	**caco**	bad	**-ia**	condition
eu-	good, well	**phon**	sound	**-ous**	having the quality of
iso-	equal	**taph**	tomb	**-y**	state of, quality, act; body, group
		thanas	death		
		therm	heat		

DIRECTIONS: In Column A, identify the elements in each word by circling roots and underlining prefixes and suffixes. Then match each word with its correct meaning from Column B.

COLUMN A

1. epi(taph) _____
2. amphibious _____
3. isothermal _____
4. euthanasia _____
5. cacophony _____

COLUMN B

a. easy and painless death

b. harsh sound; dissonance

c. inscription on a tomb or gravestone

d. related to equality or constancy of temperature

e. able to live on both land and water

DIRECTIONS: Write a complete sentence for each word in Column A. Use each word only once.

1. _____

_____

2. _____

_____

3. _____

_____

4. _____

_____

5. _____

_____

PREFIX	ROOT		SUFFIX	
pan- all	**clast**	break	**-ad**	group
	dem	people	**-ic**	like, related to
	derm	skin		
	icono*	image		
	myri	countless		
	onym	name, word		
	pachy	thick		
	pseud	false		

DIRECTIONS: In Column A, identify the elements in each word by circling roots and underlining prefixes and suffixes. Then match each word with its correct meaning from Column B.

COLUMN A

1. (myri)ad _____

2. p a n d e m i c _____

3. i c o n o c l a s t _____

4. p s e u d o n y m _____

5. p a c h y d e r m _____

COLUMN B

a. one who destroys religious images; one who challenges religious traditions

b. too numerous to count; innumerable

c. fictitious name, especially one assumed by an author

d. having a widespread effect on the population

e. mammal with thick skin

DIRECTIONS: Write a complete sentence for each word in Column A. Use each word only once.

1. _____
   _____

2. _____
   _____

3. _____
   _____

4. _____
   _____

5. _____

PREFIX		ROOT		SUFFIX	
en-	in, into	**arthr**	joint	**-ic**	like, related to
		cephal	head, brain	**-itis**	inflammation
		graph	write, written	**-ology**	study of, science
		hemat	blood	**-y**	state of, quality, act; body, group
		lith/	stone		
		litho			
		paleo*	ancient, old		

DIRECTIONS: In Column A, identify the elements in each word by circling roots and underlining prefixes and suffixes. Then match each word with its correct meaning from Column B.

COLUMN A

1. (hemat)ology ____
2. arthritis ____
3. encephalitis ____
4. Paleolithic ____
5. lithography ____

COLUMN B

a. process of printing from a metal (originally stone) plate

b. inflammation of the brain

c. related to the early Stone Age

d. study of blood and its diseases (Medical)

e. inflammation of the joint

DIRECTIONS: Write a complete sentence for each word in Column A. Use each word only once.

1. _____

_____

2. _____

_____

3. _____

_____

4. _____

_____

5. _____

_____

Extension Worksheet One

DIRECTIONS: Write the letter of the correct definition for each word.

COLUMN A	COLUMN B
1. autonomous _____	a. treatment of injury or disease with water
2. hypothermia _____	b. taking a general view of the whole subject
3. monochrome _____	c. pleasing or sweet sound
4. synoptic _____	d. a word that is opposite in meaning
5. pachyderm _____	e. belief in many gods
6. hydropathy _____	f. condition of reduced temperature
7. anachronism _____	g. made with shades of a single color
8. euphony _____	h. mammal with thick skin
9. antonym _____	i. something out of place or time
10. polytheism _____	j. self-governing; subject to one's own laws

This activity is a review of pages 1–12.

Extension Worksheet Two

DIRECTIONS: Underline the best word to complete each sentence.

1. The word frown is a/an (euonym, antonym, synonym) for the word smile.

2. The cross-country skiers were suffering from (hyperchromia, hydropathy, hypothermia) when they were found.

3. (Monotheism, Polytheism, Atheism) is a belief in many gods.

4. The high school's sports club was definitely a/an (androcentric, eugenic, mesodermic) group.

5. Organizers of the event scheduled a (synoptic, chronic, synchronous) performance of fireworks and music.

6. The telescope simplifies the task of a/an (nomographer, astronomer, geographer).

7. The tribe's (monotheism, misoneism, anachronism) kept it from progressing.

8. The new employee preferred to be (androgynous, autonomous, synonymous) rather than follow the company guidelines.

9. The historian outlined the (nomology, euphony, chronology) of events leading up to the war.

10. Researchers compared the (thermal, optical, nautical) qualities of different types of acrylic lenses.

This activity is a review of pages 1–12.

Extension Worksheet Three

DIRECTIONS: Circle the word that is spelled correctly in each group of words.

1. theapathy   theopathy   theopathie

2. optical   optikal   opptical

3. astrnaut   astronaut   astronot

4. synonem   sinonym   synonym

5. dehidrate   dyhydrate   dehydrate

6. andragyny   androginy   androgyny

7. hypodermic   hypodemic   hypdermic

8. pollychrome   polychrome   polchrome

9. misanthrop   misanthrope   missanthrope

10. epydermal   epidermal   epidurnal

This activity is a review of pages 1–12.

Extension Worksheet Four

DIRECTIONS: Write the letter of the correct definition for each word.

COLUMN A		COLUMN B
1. kleptomania	_____	a. having many sounds
2. pericardial	_____	b. related to the measurement of mental data
3. neologism	_____	c. growing on or in the ground
4. polyphonic	_____	d. new system or method of writing
5. psychometric	_____	e. situated around the heart
6. astronautics	_____	f. love of mankind
7. neography	_____	g. a new word or phrase
8. geogenous	_____	h. related to the combining or harmony of sounds
9. symphonic	_____	i. persistent craving to steal
10. philanthropy	_____	j. technology of spacecraft design and building

This activity is a review of pages 13–24.

Extension Worksheet Five

DIRECTIONS: Underline the best word to complete each sentence.

1. Once it submerged, the submarine required a (telescope, hydroscope, periscope) to search for surface vessels.

2. The overthrow of the king led to a/an (autocracy, mesocracy, ideocracy) of the merchant class.

3. A two-legged support is called a (polypod, tripod, bipod).

4. Schools use (perioptic, telephonic, psychometric) test results to place students appropriately.

5. Scientists used (neography, astrology, astrography) to pinpoint the location of the new star.

6. The author's (monograph, autograph, polygraph) on migratory habits of gray whales was printed in several scientific journals.

7. A person who writes about the earth's features is called a/an (nomographer, astronomer, geographer).

8. Speakers praised his (bibliophobia, eulogy, philanthropy) in donating the new library wing.

9. The boy's (kleptomania, bibliomania, phonophobia) was discovered when they found the missing items in his locker.

10. He was being (ideophobic, anthropopathic, gynecogenic) when he said the owls were getting even with him.

This activity is a review of pages 13–24.

Extension Worksheet Six

DIRECTIONS: Circle the word that is spelled correctly in each group of words.

1.	bibliophile	bibiopile	bibliophille
2.	philanthrupy	philanthorpy	philanthropy
3.	ulogy	eulogy	elougy
4.	peryscope	perascope	periscope
5.	polipod	polypod	polypodd
6.	ideology	ideogy	iteology
7.	monomania	momomania	mononomia
8.	pyschology	psychology	psykology
9.	phonogenik	phonogennic	phonogenic
10.	geographr	geographer	gographer

This activity is a review of pages 13–24.

Extension Worksheet Seven

DIRECTIONS: Write the letter of the correct definition for each word.

COLUMN A		COLUMN B
1. gynarchy	_____	a. testing of eyes to measure vision
2. phonogram	_____	b. rule by one person with unlimited power
3. xenophobia	_____	c. line passing through the center of a figure
4. antipathy	_____	d. letter or symbol that represents a sound
5. microbiology	_____	e. related to the effect of the mind on the body
6. psychosomatic	_____	f. lover of books
7. optometry	_____	g. fear of strangers
8. autocracy	_____	h. feeling of dislike or opposition towards something
9. diameter	_____	i. study of minute forms of life
10. bibliophile	_____	j. rule by women

This activity is a review of pages 25–37.

Extension Worksheet Eight

DIRECTIONS: Underline the best word to complete each sentence.

1. His stepdaughter's increasing (apathy, antipathy, sympathy) towards him was reflected in her rude remarks.

2. Doctors concluded her illness was (psychonomic, psychosomatic, somatogenic) and that it could not be helped with further medical treatment.

3. The study of minute forms of life is called (chronology, macrobiology, microbiology).

4. Surgeons reviewed her (micrograph, bronchogram, cardiograph) to determine how much of the tumor had invaded her lungs.

5. A person who is (hydrophobic, pathologic, hydrophilic) would be afraid to take a cruise.

6. He used a (biometer, micrometer, diameter) to measure the exact dimensions of the cell.

7. It took time for the (diachronic, diadermic, mesodermic) ointment to take effect once she had put it on.

8. A physician who wanted to become a heart surgeon would specialize in (pathology, podology, cardiology).

9. One who suffers from (hypomania, neophobia, cardiopathy) is extremely set in his ways.

10. Church and state formed a/an (gynocracy, synarchy, philogyny) in the small country.

This activity is a review of pages 25–37.

Extension Worksheet Nine

DIRECTIONS: Circle the word that is spelled correctly in each group of words.

1.	bronkioscope	bronchascope	bronchoscope
2.	somotogenic	somatogenic	somatogynic
3.	diametr	dimeter	diameter
4.	cordiogram	cardiogram	cardiogrem
5.	chronemeter	cronometer	chronometer
6.	hydorophobia	hydrfobia	hydrophobia
7.	microscopic	microsckopic	microscoppic
8.	monarkey	monarchy	monarchey
9.	antifony	antiphonie	antiphony
10.	autocracy	atrocacy	outocracy

This activity is a review of pages 25–37.

Extension Worksheet Ten

DIRECTIONS: Write the letter of the correct definition for each word.

COLUMN A

1. heliophile _____

2. pseudonym _____

3. synchronous _____

4. bicentric _____

5. pathogenic _____

6. polyarchy _____

7. telemetry _____

8. macroscopic _____

9. misogyny _____

10. amorphous _____

COLUMN B

a. related to classification of a plant or animal with two centers of origin (Biology)

b. rule by many

c. measurement of the distance of an object from an observer

d. one attracted to sunlight

e. hatred of women

f. visible to the naked eye

g. occurring at the same time

h. causing disease

i. without definite form, shapeless

j. fictitious name, especially one assumed by an author

This activity is a review of pages 38–54.

Extension Worksheet Eleven

DIRECTIONS: Underline the best word to complete each sentence.

1. The changing phases of the moon represent a (pandemic, symbiotic, cyclic) pattern.

2. The (heliophile, bibliophile, phonophile) always spent his summer vacation at the beach.

3. The forensic team was able to find (macroscopic, microscopic, cardioscopic) traces of his DNA in the tissue samples.

4. A true democracy is a form of (anarchy, polyarchy, polygamy).

5. The salamander is an/a (amorphous, amphibious, hypogenous) vertebrate.

6. Physicians discovered his illness was caused by a new (pathogenic, cyclogenic, macroscopic) strain of bacteria in raw carrots.

7. His (monophobia, dermatitis, macromania) was aggravated when he bathed with soap.

8. He used a (helioscope, phonoscope, hydroscope) to find any variations in the horn's tone.

9. An earthquake is often related to (diachronic, microscopic, hypogeous) activity.

10. The cop's whistle could not be heard over the (telemetry, polychrome, cacophony) of car horns and voices.

This activity is a review of pages 38–54.

Extension Worksheet Twelve

DIRECTIONS: Circle the word that is spelled correctly in each group of words.

1. synonymus   synonymous   sinonymous

2. misogyny   misoginy   mesogeny

3. neofobia   neaphobia   neophobia

4. cyclic   cyclick   cylic

5. sinoptic   synoptic   synobtic

6. hematology   hemitology   himatollogy

7. hypothurmia   hypothermea   hypothermia

8. myriad   myrriad   miriad

9. gensis   jeneses   genesis

10. amorfous   amorphous   amorphusx

This activity is a review of pages 38–54.

Extension Worksheet Thirteen

DIRECTIONS: Write a sentence for each of the following words.

1. anarchy _____

_____

2. chronic _____

_____

3. misanthrope _____

_____

4. hypothermia _____

_____

5. pathogenic _____

_____

6. hydrophobia _____

_____

7. antipathy _____

_____

8. monotheism _____

_____

9. symbiosis _____

_____

10. geothermal _____

_____

11. psychosis _____

_____

12. anonymous _____

_____

Latin Roots for Independent Study

DIRECTIONS: Now that you have completed the *Word Roots* activities, see how adept you have become at forming various words from any given root. Add to each word family by forming as many additional words as you can from each of these roots.

(**root** — meaning: *sample word*)

1. **prim** — first: *primordial* _____

   _____

2. **mal** — bad: *dismal* _____

   _____

3. **corp** — body: *corporation* _____

   _____

4. **lect/leg** — to read: *legible* _____

   _____

5. **fort** — strong: *fortify* _____

   _____

6. **capit** — head: *recapitulate* _____

   _____

7. **grac/grat** — pleasing, thankful: *gracious* _____

   _____

8. **sens/sent** — to feel: *resentment* _____

   _____

9. **fug** — to flee: *centrifugal* _____

   _____

10. **magn** — great: *magnitude* _____

    _____

Greek Roots for Independent Study

DIRECTIONS: Now that you have completed the *Word Roots* activities, see how adept you have become at forming various words from any given root. Add to each word family by forming as many additional words as you can from each of these roots.

(**root** — meaning: *sample word*)

1. **phot/phos** — light: *phosphene* _____

   _____

2. **tox** — poison: *intoxicated*_____

   _____

3. **soph** — wise: *philosopher* _____

   _____

4. **schiz/schism** — to split: *schizopod* _____

   _____

5. **caust/caut** — to burn: *holocaust* _____

   _____

6. **rhin** — nose: *rhinoscope* _____

   _____

7. **dyn/dynam** — power: *dynasty* _____

   _____

8. **pyr** — fire: *pyrogenic* _____

   _____

9. **ethn** — race, nation: *ethnography* _____

   _____

10. **mim** — to imitate, copy: *pantomime* _____

   _____

Anglo-Saxon (Old English) Roots for Independent Study

DIRECTIONS: Now that you have completed the *Word Roots* activities, see how adept you have become at forming various words from any given root. Add to each word family by forming as many additional words as you can from each of these roots.

(**root** — meaning: *sample word*)

1. **burn/bran** — to burn: *brandy* _____

   _____

2. **hev** — to lift: *heavy* _____

   _____

3. **stall** — place: *forestall* _____

   _____

4. **dear** — precious: *dearth* _____

   _____

5. **reck** — to heed: *reckless* _____

   _____

6. **fare** — to go: *thoroughfare* _____

   _____

7. **wit/wis** — to know: *witness* _____

   _____

8. **lik** — similar: *likeness* _____

   _____

9. **hard** (-ard SUFFIX) — hard: *billiards* _____

   _____

10. **flot** — to float: *flotsam* _____

    _____

Suggested Reference Materials for Independent Study

The general reference room of a good library contains many reference works essential to a student. Within their pages you can discover the fascinating history of word origins. Such knowledge will greatly enhance your vocabulary and spelling skills as well as improve your understanding of otherwise unfamiliar words. Learn to use your library. You will never regret it.

Below are some suggested references for independent study activities. There are also numerous reference sources online.

Adams, J. Donald, *The Magic and Mystery of Words* (New York: Holt, Rinehart and Winston, 1963).

Gove, Philip B. (ed.), *Webster's Third New International Dictionary* (Springfield, Massachusetts: Mirriam Co., 1963).

Greene, Amsel, *Word Clues* (Harper and Row Publishers, Inc., 1962).

Levitt, John and Joan, *The Spell of Words* (New York: The Philosophical Library, 1959).

Pyles, Thomas, *The Origins and Development of the English Language* (New York: Harcourt, Brace and World, 1964).

Shipley, Joseph T., *Dictionary of Word Origins* (Totowa, New Jersey: Littlefield, Adams and Company, 1964).

Skeat, Walter W., *A Concise Etymological Dictionary of the English Language* (New York: Capricorn Books, 1963).

Smith, Robert, *Dictionary of English Word-Roots* (Totowa, New Jersey: Littlefield, Adams and Company, 1966).

Webster's Encyclopedic Unabridged Dictionary of the English Language (New York: Portland House, 1989).

Answer Key

Pretest/Posttest, p. vi

1. **gynarchy**: rule by women

2. **autocosm**: self-created private world

3. **pericardial**: situated around the heart

4. **autonomous**: self-governing; subject to one's own laws

5. **misanthrope**: one who hates mankind

6. **hypothermia**: condition of reduced temperature

7. **synchronous**: occurring at the same time

8. **mesocracy**: government by the middle classes

9. **eulogy**: speech in praise of someone

10. **genocide**: killing of a race

11. **somatology**: study of human physical characteristics

12. **pathogenic**: causing disease

13. **macrobiosis**: longevity

14. **kleptomania**: persistent craving to steal

15. **micrometer**: instrument for accurately measuring small distances

16. **monotheism**: belief in one god

17. **xenophile**: lover of foreign things

18. **hydrophobia**: fear of water

19. **antisymmetric**: having opposite and irregular properties

20. **polychrome**: many-colored

Warm-Up Activity, p. vii

1. **arthritis**: inflammation of the joint

2. **pseudonym**: fictitious name, especially one assumed by an author

3. **euthanasia**: good death

4. **acrophobia**: abnormal fear of high places

5. **geographer**: one who writes about the earth's features

6. **bicentric**: related to a classification of plant or animal with two centers of origin

7. **geopathology**: study of the relationship between diseases and specific geographic locations

Page 1

1. g   chromo gen ic
2. e   chrom ium
3. b   chromo scope
4. c   hyper chrom ia
5. a   hypo chrom ia
6. f   mono chrome
7. d   poly chrome

1. monochrome
2. chromogenic
3. chromoscope
4. Chromium
5. polychrome
6. hyperchromia
7. hypochromia

Page 2

1. d   epi derm al
2. a   derm oid

3. b   hypo derm ic
4. c   meso derm ic
5. e   pachy derm

1. pachyderm
2. dermoid
3. hypodermic
4. epidermal
5. mesodermic

Page 3

1. e   ana chron ism
2. g   geo chrono logy
3. c   syn chron ous
4. f   chrono therm al
5. a   chron ic
6. d   chrono logy
7. b   chrono meter

1. chronic
2. anachronism
3. chronology
4. geochronology
5. chronothermal
6. synchronous
7. chronometer

Page 4

1. d   opto metr y
2. g   syn opt ic
3. f   opt ic al
4. b   opto phone
5. a   bi ops y
6. c   bio metr ic
7. e   bio gen ic

1. optometry
2. biopsy
3. optical
4. optophone

5. Biogenic

6. synoptic

7. biometric

Page 5

1. b chrono therm al

2. g geo therm al

3. f thermo meter

4. a hypo therm ia

5. c therm al

6. d thermo graph y

7. e thermo gen ic

1. thermometer

2. chronothermal

3. hypothermia

4. thermal

5. Thermography

6. thermogenic

7. geothermal

Page 6

1. h de hydr ate

2. f hydr ant

3. a hydro therm al

4. g hydro gen ic

5. c hydro phone

6. i hydro geo logy

7. d hydro path y

8. e hydro graph

9. b hydr onym y

1. hydrant

2. hydrophone

3. hydrogenic

4. dehydrate

5. hydrograph

6. hydrothermal

7. hydropathy

8. hydronymy

9. hydrogeology

Page 7

1. c andr oid

2. f poly andr y

3. a andro gyn ous

4. e andro centr ic

5. b andro gen

6. d andro crac y

1. Polyandry

2. androcentric

3. Androcracy

4. android

5. androgynous

6. androgen

Page 8

1. c auto crac y

2. d auto graph

3. e auto cosm

4. f auto nom ous

5. a auto gen ous

6. b auto bio graph y

1. autogenous

2. autograph

3. autonomous

4. autocracy

5. autobiography

6. autocosm

Page 9

1. a eu gen ic

2. h eu phon y

3. e eu nom y

4. f eu onym

5. g onym ous

6. i an onym ous

7. c hydr onym y

8. d syn onym ous

9. b ant onym

1. onymous

2. antonym

3. hydronymy

4. euonym

5. anonymous

6. euphony

7. eunomy

8. eugenic

9. synonymous

Page 10

1. e miso ne ism

2. d miso gyn y

3. a mis anthrope

4. b miso log ist

5. c miso gam ist

1. misogyny

2. misologist

3. misanthrope

4. misogamist

5. misoneism

Page 11

1. f a the ism

2. g mono the ism

3. e poly the ism

4. c theo logy

5. d theo path y

6. b psycho the ism

7. a theo nom y

1. theonomy

2. monotheism

3. psychotheism

4. atheism

5. theopathy

6. polytheism

7. Theology

Page 12

1. e astro nom y

2. g nomo graph er

3. c nomology
4. b autonomous
5. f nautical
6. d hydronautics
7. a astronaut
1. nomographer
2. autonomous
3. astronomy
4. astronaut
5. Nomology
6. nautical
7. hydronautics

Page 13

1. e biography
2. d macrograph
3. a graphology
4. f monograph
5. c geography
6. b neography
1. biography
2. geography
3. graphology
4. monograph
5. neography
6. macrograph

Page 14

1. c bipod
2. e podology
3. i polypod
4. g tripod
5. a pododermatitis
6. d gynecocentric
7. h gynecology
8. b gynecogenic
9. f gynecoid
1. gynecoid
2. podology

3. tripod
4. gynecology
5. gynecogenic
6. pododermatitis
7. gynecocentric
8. polypod
9. bipod

Page 15

1. f psychometric
2. d psychograph
3. e psychology
4. b psychosomatic
5. g psychosis
6. c psychonomic
7. a psychobiology
1. psychology
2. psychosis
3. psychosomatic
4. psychograph
5. psychometric
6. psychonomic
7. psychobiology

Page 16

1. c astronomy
2. d astrogeology
3. e astrology
4. b astrometry
5. a astrography
6. f astronautics
1. astrology
2. astrography
3. astrometry
4. astrogeology
5. Astronomy
6. astronautics

Page 17

1. d bibliophobia

2. f biblioklept
3. e bibliology
4. a bibliography
5. c bibliophile
6. b bibliomania
7. h kleptomania
8. i graphomania
9. g monomania
1. bibliophobia
2. biblioklept
3. bibliomania
4. graphomania
5. bibliophile
6. kleptomania
7. bibliology
8. monomania
9. bibliography

Page 18

1. c anthropoid
2. d philanthropy
3. a anthropology
4. b anthropometer
5. f anthroponomy
6. e anthropopathic
1. philanthropy
2. anthropoid
3. Anthropology
4. anthropometer
5. anthropopathic
6. anthroponomy

Page 19

1. d logic
2. e eulogy
3. f logogram
4. a logomania
5. b monolog
6. c neologism

1. monolog
2. logic
3. logomania
4. neologism
5. eulogy
6. logogram

Page 20

1. c ideocracy
2. a ideogeny
3. e ideogram
4. f ideophobia
5. d ideology
6. b ideophone

1. ideophobia
2. ideogeny
3. ideogram
4. ideology
5. ideocracy
6. ideophone

Page 21

1. e perimeter
2. d pericardial
3. c periscope
4. a perihelion
5. b perioptic

1. pericardial
2. perimeter
3. perioptic
4. perihelion
5. periscope

Page 22

1. g phonic
2. f phonogenic
3. h phonology
4. a phonopathy
5. c phonophobia

6. i homophonic
7. b polyphonic
8. d telephonic
9. e symphonic

1. phonopathy
2. symphonic
3. homophonic
4. phonogenic
5. phonology
6. polyphonic
7. phonic
8. telephonic
9. phonophobia

Page 23

1. e geochrony
2. f geology
3. d geocentric
4. c geothermal
5. b geogenous
6. a geographer

1. geographer
2. geochrony
3. geothermal
4. geogenous
5. geocentric
6. geology

Page 24

1. d mesodermic
2. e mesocracy
3. b mesotherm
4. c mesophilic
5. a mesosomatic

1. mesocracy
2. mesodermic
3. mesosomatic
4. mesotherm
5. mesophilic

Page 25

1. c psychosomatic
2. f somatogenic
3. h somatology
4. i somatometry
5. e antipathy
6. g apathy
7. b sympathy
8. a pathology
9. d psychopathology

1. Somatometry
2. sympathy
3. psychosomatic
4. antipathy
5. psychopathology
6. somatogenic
7. apathy
8. pathology
9. Somatology

Page 26

1. d dialog
2. e diameter
3. a diathermy
4. c diachronic
5. b diadermic

1. diadermic
2. dialog
3. diathermy
4. diachronic
5. diameter

Page 27

1. e antilogy
2. d antiphony
3. g antinomy
4. a anthelion
5. h antonym
6. c antipathy

7. b   anti(bio)sis

8. f   anti sym(metr)y

1. antiphony

2. anthelion

3. antibiosis

4. antonym

5. antipathy

6. antinomy

7. antilogy

8. antisymmetry

Page 28

1. h   (metr)ic

2. f   sym(metr)ic

3. g   (bio)(metr)y

4. a   (metro)logy

5. b   (opto)(metr)y

6. c   (psycho)(metr)ic

7. d   (somato)(metr)y

8. e   (metro)(nome)

1. symmetric

2. optometry

3. psychometric

4. somatometry

5. biometry

6. metronome

7. metrology

8. metric

Page 29

1. c   (broncho)(gram)

2. d   (bronch)(itis)

3. e   (broncho)(phon)y

4. a   (broncho)(gen)ic

5. b   (broncho)(scope)

1. bronchitis

2. bronchogram

3. bronchogenic

4. bronchophony

5. bronchoscope

Page 30

1. c   peri(cardi)al

2. d   (cardi)ac

3. e   (cardio)logy

4. b   (cardio)(path)y

5. a   (cardio)(graph)

1. cardiograph

2. cardiac

3. pericardial

4. cardiology

5. cardiopathy

Page 31

1. c   (micro)(bio)logy

2. d   (micro)(cosm)

3. e   (micro)(graph)

4. a   (micro)(meter)

5. b   (micro)(scop)ic

1. microscopic

2. microcosm

3. micrometer

4. microbiology

5. micrograph

Page 32

1. c   an(arch)y

2. a   tri(arch)y

3. d   mon(arch)y

4. e   (gyn)(arch)y

5. b   syn(arch)y

1. anarchy

2. gynarchy

3. triarchy

4. synarchy

5. monarchy

Page 33

1. b   (andro)(crac)y

2. c   (auto)(crac)y

3. d   (gyno)(crac)y

4. e   (ideo)(crac)y

5. a   (meso)(crac)y

1. Mesocracy

2. autocracy

3. ideocracy

4. gynocracy

5. androcracy

Page 34

1. f   (bio)(meter)

2. g   (chrono)(meter)

3. b   (hydro)(meter)

4. e   (micro)(meter)

5. d   peri(meter)

6. c   (phono)(meter)

7. a   (thermo)(meter)

1. thermometer

2. hydrometer

3. phonometer

4. perimeter

5. chronometer

6. biometer

7. micrometer

Page 35

1. c   (phono)(gram)

2. e   mono(gram)

3. d   (tele)(gram)

4. f   (cardio)(gram)

5. a   dia(gram)

6. b   (logo)(gram)

1. telegram

2. monogram

3. cardiogram

4. phonogram

5. diagram

6. logogram

Page 36

1. c cardiophobia

2. g gynophobia

3. a hydrophobia

4. e kleptophobia

5. b monophobia

6. f neophobia

7. d xenophobia

1. gynophobia

2. xenophobia

3. neophobia

4. monophobia

5. hydrophobia

6. cardiophobia

7. kleptophobia

Page 37

1. f philanthropy

2. d bibliophile

3. e philogyny

4. b xenophile

5. a philology

6. c phonophile

1. xenophile

2. philanthropy

3. philogyny

4. bibliophile

5. phonophile

6. philology

Page 38

1. c hypochromia

2. d hypodermic

3. e hypothermia

4. f hypomania

5. b hypogeous

6. a hypogenous

1. hypothermia

2. hypogenous

3. hypochromia

4. hypogeous

5. hypodermic

6. hypomania

Page 39

1. f biblioklept

2. h kleptomania

3. d kleptophobia

4. g bicycle

5. a cyclometer

6. e cyclic

7. b tricycle

8. c cyclogenic

1. cyclogenic

2. kleptophobia

3. biblioklept

4. cyclic

5. kleptomania

6. tricycle

7. cyclometer, bicycle

Page 40

1. c macrobiosis

2. d macrocosm

3. a macrograph

4. e macromania

5. b macroscopic

1. macrobiosis

2. macrograph

3. macroscopic

4. macromania

5. macrocosm

Page 41

1. e antisymmetric

2. f symbiosis

3. a sympathy

4. h symphonic

5. g synarchy

6. b synchronous

7. d synonymous

8. c synoptic

1. symbiosis

2. symphonic

3. antisymmetric

4. synchronous

5. synonymous

6. synarchy

7. synoptic

8. sympathy

Page 42

1. c heliometer

2. d helioscope

3. a heliocentric

4. e heliograph

5. b heliophile

1. helioscope

2. heliophile

3. heliometer

4. heliograph

5. heliocentric

Page 43

1. c cardioscope

2. g hydroscope

3. d telescope

4. b microscopic

5. a periscope

6. e phonoscope

7. f macroscopic

1. hydroscope

2. periscope

3. cardioscope

4. telescope

5. macroscopic

6. microscopic

7. phonoscope

Page 44

1. g polyphonic

2. e polychrome

3. a polytheism

4. f polyonymous

5. c polyarchy

6. b polygenic

7. h polycentric

8. d polygamy

1. polyonymous

2. polytheism

3. polychrome

4. polyarchy

5. Polyphonic

6. polygenic

7. polygamy

8. polycentric

Page 45

1. e androgynous

2. d gynocracy

3. b gynophobia

4. a misogyny

5. c monogynous

1. misogyny

2. Androgynous

3. gynophobia

4. monogynous

5. gynocracy

Page 46

1. b telepathy

2. g telescope

3. e telemetry

4. a telephone

5. c telegram

6. f telethermometry

7. d telegraphone

1. telescope

2. telegraphone

3. telegram

4. telemetry

5. telephone

6. telethermometry

7. telepathy

Page 47

1. e neologism

2. f neocosmic

3. d neophobia

4. c neogenesis

5. b neocracy

6. a neoanthropic

1. neophobia

2. neologism

3. neogenesis

4. neoanthropic

5. neocracy

6. neocosmic

Page 48

1. f monophobia

2. e monocentric

3. a monogenic

4. c monophonic

5. g monarchy

6. d monotheism

7. b monochrome

1. monophonic

2. monotheism

3. monarchy

4. monogenic

5. monochrome

6. monophobia

7. monocentric

Page 49

1. d pathogenic

2. f biogenic

3. a exogenous

4. e genesis

5. b genocide

6. c psychogenic

1. genocide

2. exogenous

3. pathogenic

4. genesis

5. biogenic

6. psychogenic

Page 50

1. d bicentric

2. g bichrome

3. f bicycle

4. i bipod

5. h dermatitis

6. e dermatograph

7. a dermatology

8. c dermatosis

9. b pododermatitis

1. dermatograph

2. bichrome

3. dermatosis

4. bicentric

5. bipod

6. dermatology

7. bicycle

8. dermatitis

9. pododermatitis

Page 51

1. d acrophobia

2. b agronomy

3. a amorphous

4. c entomology

5. e (hydro)(therap)y

Sentences 1–5: answers vary

Page 52

1. c epi(taph)
2. e amphi(bi)ous
3. d iso(thermal)
4. a eu(thanas)ia
5. b (caco)(phon)y

Sentences 1–5: answers vary

Page 53

1. b (myri)ad
2. d pan(dem)ic
3. a (icono)(clast)
4. c (pseud)(onym)
5. e (pachy)(derm)

Sentences 1–5: answers vary

Page 54

1. d (hemat)ology
2. e (arthr)itis
3. b en(cephal)itis
4. c (Paleo)(lith)ic
5. a (litho)(graph)y

Sentences 1–5: answers vary

Extension Worksheets

Worksheet One, p. 55

1. j
2. f
3. g
4. b
5. h
6. a
7. i
8. c
9. d
10. e

Worksheet Two, p. 56

1. antonym
2. hypothermia
3. Polytheism
4. androcentric
5. synchronous
6. geographer
7. misoneism
8. autonomous
9. chronology
10. optical

Worksheet Three, p. 57

1. theopathy (2nd)
2. optical (1st)
3. astronaut (2nd)
4. synonym (3rd)
5. dehydrate (3rd)
6. androgyny (3rd)
7. hypodermic (1st)
8. polychrome (2nd)
9. misanthrope (2nd)
10. epidermal (2nd)

Worksheet Four, p. 58

1. i
2. e
3. g
4. a
5. b
6. j
7. d
8. c
9. h
10. f

Worksheet Five, p. 59

1. periscope
2. mesocracy
3. bipod

4. psychometric
5. astrography
6. monograph
7. geographer
8. philanthropy
9. kleptomania
10. anthropopathic

Worksheet Six, p. 60

1. bibliophile (1st)
2. philanthropy (3rd)
3. eulogy (2nd)
4. periscope (3rd)
5. polypod (2nd)
6. ideology (1st)
7. monomania (1st)
8. psychology (2nd)
9. phonogenic (3rd)
10. geographer (2nd)

Worksheet Seven, p. 61

1. j
2. d
3. g
4. h
5. i
6. e
7. a
8. b
9. c
10. f

Worksheet Eight, p. 62

1. antipathy
2. psychosomatic
3. microbiology
4. bronchogram
5. hydrophobic
6. micrometer
7. diadermic

8. cardiology

9. neophobia

10. synarchy

Worksheet Nine, p. 63

1. bronchoscope (3rd)

2. somatogenic (2nd)

3. diameter (3rd)

4. cardiogram (2nd)

5. chronometer (3rd)

6. hydrophobia (3rd)

7. microscopic (1st)

8. monarchy (2nd)

9. antiphony (3rd)

10. autocracy (1st)

Worksheet Ten, p. 64

1. d

2. j

3. g

4. a

5. h

6. b

7. c

8. f

9. e

10. i

Worksheet Eleven, p. 65

1. cyclic

2. heliophile

3. microscopic

4. polyarchy

5. amphibious

6. pathogenic

7. dermatitis

8. phonoscope

9. hypogeous

10. cacophony

Worksheet Twelve, p. 66

1. synonymous (2nd)

2. misogyny (1st)

3. neophobia (3rd)

4. cyclic (1st)

5. synoptic (2nd)

6. hematology (1st)

7. hypothermia (3rd)

8. myriad (1st)

9. genesis (3rd)

10. amorphous (2nd)

Worksheet Thirteen, p. 67

Answers will vary. Accept complete sentences in which the given word makes sense according to its definition below:

1. anarchy (absence of rule)

2. chronic (continuing a long time or recurring frequently)

3. misanthrope (one who hates mankind)

4. hypothermia (condition of reduced temperature)

5. pathogenic (causing disease)

6. hydrophobia (fear of water)

7. antipathy (feeling of dislike or opposition towards something)

8. monotheism (belief in one god)

9. symbiosis (living together of two dissimilar organisms in a mutually beneficial relationship (Biology)

10. geothermal (related to the heat of the earth's interior)

11. psychosis (condition of mental illness)

12. anonymous (without a name)

Latin Roots For Independent Study, p. 68

(Answers will vary.)

Greek Roots For Independent Study , p. 69

(Answers will vary.)

Anglo-Saxon Roots For Independent Study , p. 70

(Answers will vary.)

Dictionary

Pronunciation Key

a	asp, fat, parrot	oi	oil, point, toy	l	let, yellow, ball
ā	ape, date, play	ou	out, crowd, plow	m	met, camel, trim
ä	ah, car, father	u	up, cut, color	n	not, flannel, ton
		ūr	urn, fur, deter	p	put, apple, tap
e	elf, ten, berry			r	red, port, dear
ē	even, meet, money	ə	a in ago	s	sell, castle, pass
			e in agent	t	top, cattle, hat
i	is, hit, mirror		i in sanity	v	vat, hovel, have
ī	ice, bite, high		o in comply	w	will, always, swear
			u in focus	y	yet, onion, yard
ō	open, tone, go	ər	perhaps, murder	z	zebra, dazzle, haze
ô	all, horn, law			ch	chin, catcher, arch
o͞o	ooze, tool, crew	b	bed, fable, dub	sh	she, cushion, dash
oo	look, pull, moor	d	dip, beadle, had	th	thin, nothing, truth
		f	fall, after, off	*th*	then, father, lathe
y͞oo	use, cute, few	g	get, haggle, dog	*zh*	azure, leisure
yoo	united, cure,	h	he, ahead, hotel	h	ring, anger, drink
	globule	j	joy, agile, badge	'	primary accent
		k	kill, tackle, bake	ˌ	secondary accent

PNEUMONOULTRAMICROSCOPICSILICOVOLCANOKONIOSIS

It isn't very likely that you'll come across this word in your reading, but it's fascinating in a silly way because it's so long. It certainly must be one of the longest words in English, though it's puzzling to know who would use it, since there is a much shorter word, *silicosis*, that means the same thing. It's an example of how scientists can make up new words from the ancient classical languages to describe almost anything. And it's also an example of a practice that people who are very precise in the use of language object to—the mixing of Greek and Latin roots in the same word. Below is an analysis of the word:

- **pneumono** is from Greek **pneumon**, a lung.
- **ultra** is Latin, meaning beyond, extreme or excessive, beyond the range of.
- **micro** is from Greek **micros**, small.
- **scopic** is from Greek **skopein**, to see.
- **silico** is from Latin **silex**, **silicis**, flint.
- **volcano** is from Latin **volcanus**, the god of fire, and means thrown from a volcano.
- **koni** is from Greek **konia**, dust.
- **osis** is from the same root in Latin and Greek. It means a condition, often a diseased condition.

Putting all these roots together in the right order, you have a definition of the word simply from knowing the meanings of the roots: a diseased condition of the lungs [caused by] dust from volcanic flint [so fine as to be] beyond the range of [an instrument which] sees very small [things].[1]

[1] Helene and Charlton Laird, *The Tree of Language* [London, England: 1957]

GREEK AND LATIN PREFIXES

a-   Greek — away, from; not, without
amorphous [ə-môr´-fəs] without definite form, shapeless
apathy [ap´-ə-thē] lack of feeling
atheism [ā´-thē-iz´-m] denial of the existence of a god

amphi-   Greek — both, around
amphibious [am-fib´-ē-əs] able to live on both land and water

an-   Greek — not, without
anarchy [an´-ər-kē] absence of rule
anonymous [ă-nän´-ə-məs] without a name

ana-   Greek — back, against
anachronism [ə-nak´-rə-niz´-m] something out of place or time

ant-   Greek — against, opposite
anthelion [ant´-hēl´-y-ən] bright spot occurring opposite the sun
antonym [an´-tə-nim´] word that is opposite in meaning

anti-   Greek — against, opposite
antibiosis [an´-ti-bī-ō´-sis] association between organisms which is injurious to one of them
antilogy [an-til´-ə-jē] contradiction in terms or ideas
antinomy [an-tin´-ə-mē] opposition of one law to another
antipathy [an-tip´-ə-thē] feeling of dislike or opposition toward something
antiphony [an-tif´-ə-nē] opposition of sounds between two groups
antisymmetric [an´-ti-si-met´-rik] having opposite and irregular properties
antisymmetry [an´-ti-si´-met-rē] opposing, irregular properties

bi-   Latin — two
bicentric [bī´-sen´-trik] related to a classification of plant or animal with two centers of origin (Biology)
bichrome [bī-krōm´] having two colors
bicycle [bī´-si-k'l] vehicle with two wheels
bipod [bī´-päd´] two-legged support

de-   Latin — from, away, down, apart; not
dehydrate [dē-hī´-drāt] to take water from

dia-   Greek — through, across
diachronic [dī´-ə-krän´-ik] considering phenomena, such as language, as they change over time
diadermic [dī´-ə-dər´-mik] acting through the skin
diagram [dī´-ə-gram´] drawing or design showing the relationship between parts of a whole
dialog [dī´-ə-lôg´] conversation between two or more persons
diameter [dī-am´-ə-tər] line passing through the center of a figure
diathermy [dī´-ə-thūr´-mē] generation of heat in body tissue by electric current (Medical)

en-   Greek — in, into
encephalitis [en-sef´-ə-lī´-tis] inflammation of the brain

epi-   Greek — on, outside
epidermal [ep´-ə-dūr´-m'l] related to the outer layer of skin
epitaph [ep´-ə-taf´] inscription on a tomb or gravestone

eu-   good, well
eugenic [yoo-jen´-ik] of good birth
eulogy [yoo´-lə-jē] speech in praise of someone
eunomy [yoo´-nə-mē] civil order under good laws; good government
euonym [yoo´-ə-nim´] well-suited name
euphony [yoo´-fə-nē] pleasing or sweet sound
euthanasia [yoo´-thə-na´-zhə] good death, easy and painless death

exo-   Greek — outside
exogenous [ek-säj´-ə-nəs] caused by a factor or agent outside the organism (Medical)

hyper-   Greek — over, above
hyperchromia [hī´-pər-krō´-mē-ə]

excessive pigmentation (color), as of the skin (Biology)

hypo-   Greek — under, below
hypochromia [hī´-pə-krō´-mē-ə] lack of color
hypodermic [hī´-pə-dūr´-mik] under the skin
hypogenous [hī-päj´-ə-nəs] growing on the underside (Botany)
hypogeous [hī´-pə-jē´-əs] happening underground (Geology)
hypomania [hī´-pə-mā´-nē-ə] mild form of psychosis indicated by elevated mood (Psychology)
hypothermia [hī´-pə-thūr´-mē-ə] condition of reduced temperature

iso-   Greek — equal
isothermal [ī´-sə-thūr´-m´l] related to equality or constancy of temperature

mon-   Greek — one
monarchy [män´-ər-kē] rule by one person

mono-   Greek — one
monocentric [mä´-nə-sen´-trik] having a single center
monochrome [män´-ə-krōm] made of shades of a single color
monogenic [män´-ə-jen´-ik] having a single or common origin
monogram [män´-ə-gram´] one or more single letters (such as initials) used to represent a name
monograph [män´-ə-graf´] detailed scholarly article or book on a single topic
monogynous [mə-näj´-ə-nəs] having only one wife at a time
monolog [män´-ə-lôg] long speech given by one person
monomania [män´-ə-mā´-nē-ə] obsession with one object or idea
monophobia [män´-ə-fō´-bē-ə] abnormal fear of being alone
monophonic [män´-ə-fän´-ik] having one sound
monotheism [män´-ə-thē´-iz-m] belief in one god

pan-   Greek— all
pandemic [pan-dem´-ik] having a widespread effect on the population

peri-   Greek — around, surrounding
pericardial [per´-ə-kär´-dē-´l] situated around the heart (Biology)
perihelion [per´-ə-hē´-lē-ən] point closest to the sun in a planet's orbit (Astronomy)
perimeter [pə-rim´-ə-tər] circumference or distance around a figure
perioptic [per´-ē-äp´-tik] situated about or surrounding the eyeball (Medicial)
periscope [per´-ə-skōp´] instrument for viewing the surrounding area, especially objects not in the direct line of sight

sym-   Greek — with, together
antisymmetric [an´-ti-si-met´-rik] having opposite and irregular properties
antisymmetry [an´-ti-si´-met-rē] opposing, irregular properties
symbiosis [sim´-bī-ō´-sis] living together of two dissimilar organisms in a mutually beneficial relationship (Biology)
symmetric [si-met´-rik] having corresponding parts the same in size and form
sympathy [sim´-pə-thē] supporting another's viewpoint, ability to share another's feelings
symphonic [sim-fän´-ik] related to the combining or harmony of sounds

syn-   Greek — with, together
synarchy [sin´-ər-kē] joint rule
synchronous [syn´-krə-nəs] occurring at the same time
synonym [sin´-ə-nim] word with a similar meaning
synonymous [si-nän´-ə-məs] having a similar meaning (Linguistics)
synoptic [si-näp´-tik] taking a general view of the whole subject

tri-   Greek — three
triarchy [trī´-är-kē] rule or government by three persons
tricycle [trī´-si-k´l] vehicle with three wheels
tripod [trī´-päd] three-legged stand

GREEK ROOTS

acro   height, top
acrophobia [ak´-rə-fō´-bē-ə] abnormal fear of high places

agro   field
agronomy [ə-grän´-ə-mē] management of farm land

andr   man, male
android [an´-droid] humanlike robot
polyandry [päl´-ē-an´-drē] practice of having two or more husbands at one time

andro   (combining form) man, male
androcentric [an´-drō-sen´-trik] centered around male interests
androcracy [an´-dräk´-rə-sē] political and social rule by men
androgen [an´-drə-jən] male sex hormone
androgynous [an-dräj´-ə-nəs] having both male and female characteristics

anthrop   mankind, man
anthropoid [an´-thrə-poid´] resembling man
neoanthropic [nē´-ō-an-thräp´-ik] belonging to the same species as recent man
philanthropy [fi-lan´-thrə-pē] love of mankind

anthrope   mankind, man
misanthrope [mis´-ən-thrōp´] one who hates mankind

anthropo   (combining form) mankind, man
anthropology [an'-thrə-päl´-ə-jē] study of mankind
anthropometer [an´-thrə-päm´-ə-dər] device used to measure the proportions of the human body
anthroponomy [an´-thrə-pän´-ə-mē] natural laws of human development as they relate to the environment
anthropopathic [an´-thrə-pō-path´-ik] relating human feelings to something not human

arch   first, chief, rule
anarchy [an´-ər-kē] absence of rule
gynarchy [gin´-ər´-kē] rule by women
monarchy [män´-ər-kē] rule by one person
polyarchy [pä´-lē-ər´-kē] rule by many
synarchy [sin´-ər-kē] joint rule
triarchy [trī´-är-kē] rule or government by three persons

arthr   joint
arthritis [är-thrit´-is] inflammation of the joint

astro   (combining form) star, heavens
astrogeology [as´-trə-jē-äl´-ə-jē] study of the structure and composition of heavenly bodies
astrography [ə-sträg´-rə-fē] mapping of the planets and stars
astrology [a-sträl´-ə-jē] study of the influence of stars on humans
astrometry [ə-sträm´-ə-trē] measurement of the positions and distances of stars
astronaut [as´-trə-nôt´] one who travels throughout the universe
astronautics [as´-trə-nôt´-iks] technology of spacecraft design and building
astronomy [ə -strän´-ə-mē] science dealing with the order of celestial bodies

auto   (combining form) self
autobiography [ôt´-ə-bi-ä´-grə-fē] person's life history written by himself
autocosm [ôd´-ō-käz´-əm] self-created private world
autocracy [ô-tä´-krə-sē] rule by one person with unlimited power
autogenous [ô-täj´-ə-nəs] produced from within, self-generating (Biology)
autograph [ôt´-ə-graf´] person's signature

autonomous [ô-tän´-ə-məs] self-governing; subject to one's own laws

bi life

amphibious [am-fib´-ē-əs] able to live on both land and water

biopsy [bī´-äp'-sē] removal and examination of tissue from a living body

biblio book

bibliography [bib´-lē-äg´-rə-fē] list of books

biblioklept [bib´-lē-ə-klept´] one who steals books

bibliology [bib´-lē-äl´-ə-jē] history and science of books as physical objects

bibliomania [bib´-lē-ə-mā´-nē-ə] excessive preoccupation with books

bibliophile [bib´-lē-ə-fīl´] lover of books

bibliophobia [bib´-lē-ə-fō´-bē-ə] dread or hatred of books

bio life

antibiosis [an´-ti-bī-ō´-sis] association between organisms which is injurious to one of them

autobiography [ôt´-ə-bī-ä´-grə-fē] person's life story written by himself

biogenic [bī´-ō-jen´-ik] produced by the action of living organisms

biography [bī-äg´-rə-fē] written story of someone's life

biometer [bī-äm´-ə-tər] device that measures carbon dioxide given off by living matter (Biology)

biometric [bi-ə-me´-trik] related to statistical analysis of biological observations and phenomena

biometry [bī-äm´-ə-trē] statistical analysis of biological observations and phenomena

macrobiosis [mak´-rō-bī-ō´-sis] longevity

microbiology [mī´-krō-bī-äl´-ə-jē] study of minute forms of life

psychobiology [sī´-kō-bī-äl´-ə-jē] study of relationship between biological processes and behavior

symbiosis [sim´-bī-ō´-sis] living together of two dissimilar organisms in a mutually beneficial relationship (Biology)

bronch throat, airways

bronchitis [brän-kīt´-is] inflammation of the air passages

broncho throat, airways

bronchogenic [brän´-kō-jen´-ik] originating from the air passages of the lungs (Medical)

bronchogram [brän´-kō-gram´] an X-ray of the air passages

bronchophony [brän´-käf´-ə-nē] sound of the voice heard through the stethoscope over healthy lungs (Medical)

bronchoscope [brän´-kə-skōp´] thin tube which enables a doctor to see into the airways

caco bad

cacophony [kə-käf´-ə-nē] harsh sound, dissonance

cardi heart

cardiac [kär´-dē-ak´] pertaining to the heart

pericardial [per´-ə-kär´-dē´-l] situated around the heart (Biology)

cardio heart

cardiogram [kär´-dē-ə-gram´] record of the heart's movements

cardiograph [kär´-dē-ə-graf´] instrument that graphically records the heart's movements

cardiology [kär´-dē-äl´-ə-jē] study of the heart

cardiopathy [kär´-dē-äp´-ə-thē] disease of the heart (Medical)

cardiophobia [kär´-dē-ə-fō´-bē-ə] abnormal fear of heart disease

cardioscope [kär´-dē-ə-skōp´] instrument for viewing the interior of the heart

centr center

androcentric [an´-drō-sen´-trik] centered around male interests

bicentric [bī´-sen´-trik] related to a classification of plant or animal with two centers of origin (Biology)

geocentric [jē´-ō-sen´-trik] related to the earth's center; earth-centered

gynecocentric [gīn´-ə-kō-sen´-trik] causing female characteristics

heliocentric [hē´-lē-ō-sen´-trik] centered on the sun

monocentric [mä´-nə-sen´-trik] having a single center

polycentric [päl´-i-sen´-trik] having more than one center (Biology); having multiple centers of control (Political Science)

cephal   head, brain

encephalitis [en-sef´-ə-lī´-tis] inflammation of the brain

chrom   color

chromium [krō´-me-əm] element used for making pigments

hyperchromia [hī´-pər-krō´-mē-ə] excessive pigmentation [color], as of the skin

hypochromia [hī´-pə-krō´-mē-ə] lack of color

chrome   color

bichrome [bī-krōm´] having two colors

monochrome [män´-ə-krōm] made of shades of a single color

polychrome [päl´-i-krōm] many-colored

chromo   color

chromogenic [kro´-mə-jen´-ik] producing color

chromoscope [krō´-mə-skōp´] optical instrument used to study various properties of color, including value and intensity

chron   time

anachronism [ə-nak´-rə-niz´-m] something out of place or time

chronic [krän´-ik] continuing a long time or recurring frequently

diachronic [dī´-ə-krän´-ik] considering phenomena, such as

languages, as they change over time

geochrony [jē´-äk´-rə-nē] system of time divisions used in the study of the earth

synchronous [sin´-krə-nəs] occurring at the same time

chrono   time

chronology [krə-näl´-ə-jē] science of determining the order in which things occur

chronometer [krə-näm´-ə-tər] timekeeping device of great accuracy, esp. used in measuring longitude

chronothermal [krə´-nä-thūr´-m´l] relating to both time and temperature

geochronology [jē´-ō-krə-näl´-ə-je] study of the ages of geologic events

clast   break

iconoclast [i-kän´-ə-klast´] one who destroys religious images; one who challenges religious traditions

cosm   universe, harmony

autocosm [ôd´-ō-käz-əm] self-created private world

macrocosm [mak´-rə-käz´-m] big world or universe

microcosm [mī´-krə-käz´-m] small world; a miniature copy of a larger whole

neocosmic [nē´-ō-käz´-mik] related to the universe in its present state

crac   government, rule

androcracy [an´-dräk´-rə-sē] political and social rule by men

autocracy [ô-tä´-krə-sē] rule by one person with unlimited power

gynocracy [ji´-näk´-rə-sē] government by women

ideocracy [īdē´-äk´-rə-sē] government based on an all-embracing idea or theory

mesocracy [mə-zäk´-rə-sē] government by the middle classes

neocracy [nē´-äk´-rə-sē] government by those new to government

cycl   circle

cyclic [sī´-klik] occurring or repeating in cycles

cycle	circle	**gam**	united, joined

cycle circle

bicycle [bī´-si k´l] vehicle with two wheels

tricycle [trī´-si-k´l] vehicle with three wheels

cyclo circle

cyclogenic [sī´-klä-jen´-ik] relating to life cycles

cyclometer [sī´-kläm´-ə-tər] device that measures number of rotations of a wheel to indicate distance travelled

dem people

pandemic [pan-dem´-ik] having a widespread effect on the population

derm skin

dermoid [dūr´-moid] resembling skin (Medical)

diadermic [dī´-ə-dər´-mik] acting through the skin

epidermal [ep´-ə-dūr´-m´l] related to the outer layer of skin (Biology)

hypodermic [hī´-pə-dūr´-mik] under the skin

mesodermic [mes´-ə-dūr´-mik] related to the middle layer of skin (Biology)

pachyderm [pak´-ə-durm´] mammal with thick skin

dermat skin

dermatitis [dūr´-mə-tī´-tis] inflammation of the skin

dermatosis [dūr´-mə-tō´-sis] disease of the skin

pododermatitis [pä-dō-dūr´-mə-tīt´-is] inflammation of the skin tissue of the foot

dermato skin

dermatograph [dūr´-mat´-ə-graf] instrument for producing markings on skin

dermatology [dūr´-mə-täl´-ə-jē] study of skin

entom insect

entomology [en´-tə-mäl´-ə-jē] branch of zoology that deals with insects

gam united, joined

misogamist [mi-säg´-ə-məst] one who hates marriage

polygamy [pə-lig´-ə-mē] having more than one spouse at the same time

ge earth, ground

hypogeous [hī´-pə-jē´-äs] happening underground (Geology)

gen cause, birth, race, produce

androgen [an´-drə-jän] male sex hormone

autogenous [ô-täj´-ə-nəs] produced from within, self-generating (Biology)

biogenic [bī´-ō-jen´-ik] produced by the action of living organisms (Geology)

bronchogenic [brän- kō-jen´-ik] originating from the air passages of the lungs (Medical)

chromogenic [krō´-mə-jen´-ik] producing color

cyclogenic [sī´-klä-jen´-ik] relating to life cycles

eugenic [yoo-jen´-ik] of good birth

exogenous [ek-säj´-ə-nəs] caused by a factor or agent outside the organism (Medical)

genesis [jen´-ə-sis] beginning or birth of something

geogenous [jē´-äj´-ə-nəs] growing on or in the ground

gynecogenic [gīnə´-kō-jen´-ik] causing female characteristics

hydrogenic [hī´-drə-jen´-ik] caused by the action of water (Geology)

hypogenous [hī-päj´-ə-nəs] growing on the underside (Botany)

ideogeny [īd´-ē-äj´-ə-nē] origin of ideas (Philosophy)

neogenesis [nē´-ō-jen´-ə-sis] new formation [as of tissue]

pathogenic [path´-ə-jen´-ik] causing disease

phonogenic [fō´-nə-jen´-ik] suitable for producing sound

polygenic [päl´-i-jen´-ik] coming from multiple genes

psychogenic [sī´-kō-jen´-ik] originating in the mind

somatogenic [sō´-mə-tə-jen´-ik] originating in the cells of the body (Medical)

thermogenic [thūr´-mə-jen´-ik] producing heat (Physiology)

geno   cause, birth, race, produce

genocide [jen´-ə-sīd´] killing of a race

geo   earth, ground

astrogeology [as´-trə-jē-äl´-ə-je] study of the structure and composition of heavenly bodies

geocentric [jē´-ō-sen´-trik] related to the earth's center; earth-centered

geochronology [jē´-ō-krə-näl´-ə-jē] study of the ages of geologic events

geochrony [jē-äk´-rə-nē] system of time divisions used in the study of the earth

geogenous [jē-äj´-ə-nəs] growing on or in the ground

geographer [jē-äg´-rə-fər] one who writes about the earth's features

geography [jē-äg´-rə-fē] description of the the earth's features

geology [jē-äl´-ə-jē] study of the earth's structure

geopathology [jē´-äl-path-äl-ə-jē] study of the relationship between diseases and specific geographic locations

geothermal [jē´-ō-thūr´-m'l] related to the heat of the earth's interior

hydrogeology [hī´-drə-jē-äl´-ə-jē] study of subsurface water movement through rocks

gra   write, written

telegraphone [ti leg´ rä fōn] early device for recording sound

gram   write, written

bronchogram [brän´-kō-gram´] X-ray of the air passages

cardiogram [kär´-dē-ə-gram´] record of the heart's movements

diagram [dī-ə-gram´] drawing or design showing the relationship

between parts of a whole

ideogram [id´-ē-ə-gram´] graphic symbol used to represent a concept or word

logogram [lôg´-ə-gram´] letter or symbol used to represent an entire word

monogram [män´-ə-gram´] one or more single letters (such as initials) used to represent a name

phonogram [fō´-nə-gram´] letter or symbol that represents a sound

telegram [tel´-ə-gram´] written message sent from a distance

graph   write, written

astrography [ə-sträg´-rə-fē] mapping of the planets and stars

autobiography [ôt´-ə-bī-ä´-grə-fē] person's life story written by himself

autograph [ôt´-ə-graf´] person's signature

bibliography [bib´-lē-äg´-rə-fē] list of books

biography [bī-äg´-rə-fē] written story of someone's life

cardiograph [kär´-dē-ə-graf´] instrument that graphically records the heart's movements

dermatograph [dūr´-mat´-ə-graf] instrument for producing markings on skin

geographer [jē-äg´-rə-fər] one who writes about the earth's features

geography [jē-äg´-rə-fē] description of the earth's features

heliograph [hē´-lē-ə-graf´] device for telegraphing by means of the sun's rays

hydrograph [hī´-drə-graf´] diagram of the levels or amount of water flow in a river

lithography [li-thäg´-rə-fē] process of printing from a metal (originally stone) plate

macrograph [ma´-krə-graf´] image that is equal to or larger than the object

micrograph [mī´-krə-graf´] picture or drawing of something seen through a microscope

monograph [män´-ə-graf´] detailed scholarly article or book on a single topic

neography [nē-äg´-rə-fē] new system or method of writing

nomographer [nō-mäg´-rə-fər] one who writes laws

psychograph [sī´-kə-graf´] chart of an individual's personality traits

thermography [thär-mäg´-rə-fē] recording a visual image of body heat using infrared devices (Medical)

grapho   write, written

graphology [graf-äl´-ə-jē] study of handwriting

graphomania [graf´-ə-mā´-nē-ə] obsessive desire to write

gyn   woman, female

androgynous [an-dräj´-ə-nəs] having both male and female characteristics

gynarchy [gin´-är-kē] rule by women

misogyny [mi-säj´-ə-nē] hatred of women

monogynous [mə-näj´-ə-nəs] having only one wife at a time

philogyny [fi-läj´-ə-nē] fondness for women

gynec   woman, female

gynecoid [gin´-ə-koid´] physically resembling the female

gyneco   woman, female

gynecocentric [gīn´-ə-kō-sen´-trik] centered around the female point of view

gynecogenic [gīn´-ə-kō-jen´-ik] causing female characteristics

gynecology [gī´-nə-käl´-ə-jē] science of women's disorders (Medical)

gyno   woman, female

gynocracy [gi-näk´-rə-sē] government by women

gynophobia [gin´-ə-fō´-bē-ə] fear of women

heli   sun

anthelion [ant´-hēl´-y-ən] bright spot occurring opposite the sun

perihelion [per´-ə-hē´-lē-ən] point closest to the sun in a planet's orbit (Astronomy)

helio   sun

heliocentric [hē´-lē-ō-sen´-trik] centered on the sun

heliograph [hē´-lē-ə-graf´] device for telegraphing by means of the sun's rays

heliometer [hē´-lē-äm´-ə-tər] device originally designed to measure the sun's diameter and the angles between stars

heliophile [hē´-lēə-fil´] one attracted to sunlight

helioscope [hē´-lē-ə-skōp´] device for viewing the sun

hemat   blood

hematology [hē´-mə-täl´-ə-jē] study of blood and its diseases (Medical)

homo   (combining form) same

homophonic [häm´-ə-fän´-ik] having the same sound

hydr   water

dehydrate [dē-hī´-drāt] to take water from

hydrant [hī´-drənt] device for drawing water

hydro   (combining form) water

hydrogenic [hī´-drə-jen´-ik] caused by the action of water (Geology)

hydrogeology [hī´-drə-jē-äl´-ə-jē] study of subsurface water movement through rock

hydrograph [hī´-drə-graf´] diagram of the levels or amount of water flow in a river

hydrometer [hī-dräm´-ə-tər] instrument for measuring the specific gravity of liquids

hydronautics [hī´-drə-nôt´-iks] technology related to the development of deep submersible vehicles

hydronymy [hī-drän´-ə-mē] naming or names of bodies of water

hydropathy [hī-dräp´-ə-thē] treatment of injury or disease with water (Medical)

hydrophobia [hī´-drə-fō´-bē-ə] fear of water

hydrophone [hī´-drə-fōn´] receiver for listening to sound transmitted through water

hydroscope [hī´-drə-skōp´] device for viewing objects below the surface of water

hydrotherapy [hī´-drō-ther´-ə pē] treatment of disease or injury by the use of baths, etc.

hydrothermal [hī´-drō-thūr´-məl] of or relating to hot water

icono   (combining form) image

iconoclast [i-kän´-ə-klast´] one who destroys religious images; one who challenges religious traditions

ideo   (combining form) idea

ideocracy [id´-ē-äk´-rə-sē] government based on all-embracing idea or theory

ideogeny [id´-ē-äj´-ə-nē] origin of ideas (Philosophy)

ideogram [id´-ē-ə-gram´] graphic symbol used to represent a concept or word

ideology [i´-dē-äl´-ə-jē] system of interrelated social beliefs and values

ideophobia [i-dē-ə-fō´-bē-ə] fear or distrust of ideas

ideophone [i´-dē-ə-fōn´] sound or pattern of sounds used to represent a concept

klept   to steal

biblioklept [bib´-lē-ə-klept´] one who steals books

klepto   to steal

kleptomania [klep´-tə-mā´-nē-ə] persistent craving to steal

kleptophobia [klep´-tə-fō´-bē-ə] fear of stealing (or being stolen from)

lith   stone

Paleolithic [pā´-lē-ə-lith´-ik] related to the early Stone Age

litho   stone

lithography [li-thäg´-rə-fē] process of printing from a metal (originally stone) plate

log   word, reason

antilogy [an-til´-ə-jē] contradiction in terms or ideas

dialog [dī´-ə-lôg´] conversation between two or more persons

eulogy [yōō´-lə-jē] speech in praise of someone

logic [läj´-ik] related to theory of reasoning (Philosophy)

misologist [mi-säl´-ə-jist] one who hates reasoning

monolog [män´-ə-lôg´] long speech given by one person

neologism [nē-äl´-ä-jiz´-m] new word or phrase

philology [fi-läl´-ə-jē] study of a culture's language and literature (literally, a fondness for words)

logo   word, reason

logogram [lôg´-ä-gram´] symbol used to represent an entire word

logomania [lôg´-ä-mā´-nē-ä] abnormal talkativeness

macro   (combining form) large, great

macrobiosis [mak´-rō-bī´-ō´-sis] longevity

macrocosm [mak´-rə-käz´-m] big world or universe

macrograph [ma´-krə-graf] image that is equal to or larger than the object

macromania [mak´-rō-mā´-nē-ə] delusion that things are larger than they really are

macroscopic [mak´-rə-skäp´-ik] visible to the naked eye

mania   intense craving, loss of reason

bibliomania [bib´-lē-ə-mā´-nē-ə] excessive preoccupation with books

graphomania [graf´-ə-mā´-nē-ə] obsessive desire to write

hypomania [hī´-pə-mā´-nē-ə] mild form of psychosis indicated by an elevated mood (Psychology)

kleptomania [klep´-tə-mā´-nē-ə] persistent craving to steal

logomania [lôg´-ə-mā´-nē-ə] abnormal talkativeness

macromania [mak´-rō-mā´-nē-ə] delusion that things are larger than they really are

monomania [män-ə-mā´-nē-ə] obsession with one object or idea

meso (combining form) middle

mesocracy [mə-zäk´-rə-sē] government by the middle classes

mesodermic [mes´-ə-dūr´-mik] related to the middle layer of skin (Biology)

mesophilic [mez´-ə-fil´-ik] thriving in a moderate environment (Biology)

mesosomatic [mez-ō´-sō-mat´-ik] related to the middle region of the body of various invertebrates (Zoology)

mesotherm [mez´-ō-thərm´] plant that requires a moderate degree of heat (Botany)

meter measure

anthropometer [an´-thrə-päm´-ə-tər] device used to measure the proportions of the human body

biometer [bī-äm´-ə-tər] device that measures carbon dioxide given off by living matter (Biology)

chronometer [krə-näm´-ə-tər] timekeeping device of great accuracy, especially. used in measuring longitude

cyclometer [sī´-kläm´-ə-tər] device that measures number of rotations of a wheel to indicate distance travelled

diameter [dī-am´-ə-tər] line passing through the center of a figure

heliometer [hē´-lē-äm´-ə-tər] device originally designed to measure the sun's diameter and the angles between stars

hydrometer [hī-dräm´-ə-tər] instrument for measuring the specific gravity of liquids

micrometer [mī-kräm´-ə-tər] instrument for accurately measuring small distances

perimeter [pä-rim´-ə-tər] circumference or distance around a figure

phonometer [fō näm´-ə-tər] instrument which measures the intensity of sound

thermometer [thər-mäm´-ə-tər] instrument which measures heat

metr measure

antisymmetric [an´-ti-si-met´-rik] having opposite and irregular properties

antisymmetry [an´-ti-si´-met-rē] opposing, irregular properties

astrometry [ə-sträm´-ə-trē] measurement of the positions and distances of stars

biometric [bi-ə-me´-trik] related to statistical analysis of biological observations and phenomena

biometry [bī-äm´-ə-trē] statistical analysis of biological observations and phenomena

metric [met´-rik] related to the system of meters

optometry [äp-täm´-ə-trē] testing of eyes to measure vision

psychometric [sī´-kə-met´-rik] related to the measurement of mental data

somatometry [sō´-mə-täm´-ə-trē] related to body measurement (Anthropology)

symmetric [si-met´-rik] having corresponding parts the same in size and form

telemetry [tə-lem´-ə-trē] measurement of the distance of an object from an observer

telethermometry [tel´-ə-thər-mäm´-ə-trē] process for taking remote temperature

metro measure

metrology [me-träl´-ə-jē] science of weights and measures

metronome [met´-rə-nōm] device used to measure rhythm

micro	(combining form) small
	microbiology [mī´-krō-bī-äl´-ə-jē] study of minute forms of life
	microcosm [mī´-krə-käz´-m] small world; a miniature copy of a larger whole
	micrograph [mī´-krə-graf´] picture or drawing of something seen through a microscope
	micrometer [mī-kräm´-ə-tər] instrument for accurately measuring small distances
	microscopic [mī´-krə-skäp´-ik] too small to be seen by the naked eye
mis	hate
	misanthrope [mis´-ən-thrōp´] one who hates mankind
miso	(combining form) hate
	misogamist [mi-säg´-ə-məst] one who hates marriage
	misogyny [mi-säj´-ə-nē] hatred of women
	misologist [mi-säl´-ə-jist] one who hates reasoning
	misoneism [mis´-ō-nē´-iz´-m] hatred of innovation or change
morph	form
	amorphous [ə-môr´-fəs] without definite form, shapeless
myri	countless
	myriad [mir´-ē-əd] too numerous to count; innumerable
naut	sailor, ship
	astronaut [as´-trə-nôt´] one who travels throughout the universe
	astronautics [as´-trə-nôt´-iks] technology of spacecraft design and building
	hydronautics [hī´-drə-nôt´-iks] technology related to the development of deep submersible vehicles
	nautical [nôt´-i-kəl] related to ships or sailing

ne	new, recent
	misoneism [mis´-ō-nē´-iz´-m] hatred of innovation or change
neo	(combining form) new, recent
	neoanthropic [nē´-ō-an-thräp´-ik] belonging to the same species as recent man (Anthropology)
	neocosmic [nē´-ō-käz´-mik] related to the universe in its present state
	neocracy [nē´-äk´-rə-sē] government by those new to government
	neogenesis [nē´-ō-jen´-ə-sis] new formation (as of tissue)
	neography [nē-äg´-rə-fē] new system or method of writing
	neologism [nē-äl´-ə-jiz´-m] new word or phrase
	neophobia [nē´-ə-fō´-bē-ə] fear of change or new things
nom	name, law, custom, order
	agronomy [ə-grän´-ə-mē] management of farm land
	anthroponomy [an´-thrə-pän´-ə-mē] natural laws of human development as they relate to the environment
	antinomy [an-tin´-ə-mē] opposition of one law to another
	astronomy [ə-strän´-ə-mē] science dealing with the order of celestial bodies
	autonomous [ô-tän´-ə-məs] self-governing, subject to one's own laws
	eunomy [yōō´-nə-mē] civil order under good laws; good government
	psychonomic [sī´-kə-näm´-ik] related to the laws of behavior and cognitive function
	theonomy [thē-ä´-nə-mē] governed by a god; divine rule
nome	name, law, custom, order
	metronome [met´-rə-nōm´] device used to measure rhythm
nomo	name, law, custom, order
	nomographer [nō-mäg´-rə-fər] one who writes laws (History)
	nomology [nō-mäl´-ə-jē] science of laws and lawmaking (Philosophy)

onym name, word

anonymous [ə-nän´-ə-məs] without a name

antonym [an´-tə-nim´] word that is opposite in meaning

euonym [yoo̅´-ə-nim´] well-suited name

hydronymy [hī-drän´-ə-mē] naming or names of bodies of water

onymous [än´-ə-məs] having the writer's name

polyonymous [päl´-ē-än´-ə-məs] having many names

pseudonym [soo̅´-də-nim´] fictitious name, especially one assumed by an author

synonym [sin´-ə-nim] word with a similar meaning

synonymous [si-nän´-ə-məs] having a similar meaning (Linguistics)

ops eye, vision

biopsy [bī´-äp´-sē] removal and examination of tissue from a living body

opt eye, vision

optical [äp´-ti-kəl] pertaining to the eye, vision

perioptic [per-ē-äpt´-ik] situated about or surrounding the eyeball (Medical)

synoptic [si-näp´-tik] taking a general view of the whole subject

opto eye, vision

optometry [äp-täm´-ə-trē] testing of eyes to measure vision

optophone [äp´-tə-fōn´] device used by the visually impaired to convert written text into sounds

pachy thick

pachyderm [pak´-ə-durm´] mammal with thick skin

paleo (combining form) ancient, old

Paleolithic [pā´-lē-ə-lith´-ik] related to the early Stone Age

path feeling, disease

anthropopathic

[an´-thrə-pō-path´ik] relating human feelings to something not human

antipathy [an-tip´-ə-thē] feeling of dislike or opposition towards something

apathy [ap´-ə-thē] lack of feeling

cardiopathy [kär´-dē-äp´-ə thē] disease of the heart

hydropathy [hī-dräp´-ə-thē] treatment of injury or disease with water (Medical)

phonopathy [fə-näp´-ə-thē] speech disorder

sympathy [sim´-pə-thē] supporting another's viewpoint, ability to share another's feelings

telepathy [tə-lep´-ə-thē] communication between minds

theopathy [thē-äp´-ə-thē] intense absorption in religious devotion

patho feeling, disease

geopathology [jē´-äl-path-äl-ə-jē] study of the relationship between diseases and specific geographic locations

pathogenic [path´-ə-jen´-ik] causing disease

pathology [pä-thäl´-ə-jē] study of disease

psychopathology
[sī´-kō-pa-thäl´-ə-jē] study of mental disease

phil love, loving

mesophilic [mez´-ə-fil´-ik] thriving in a moderate environment (Biology)

philanthropy [fi-lan´-thrə-pē] love of mankind

phile love, loving

bibliophile [bib´-lē-ə-fīl´] lover of books

heliophile [hē´-lē-ə-fīl´] one attracted to sunlight

phonophile [fo´-nə-fīl´] lover and collector of phonograph records

xenophile [zen´-ə-fīl´] lover of foreign things

philo   love, loving

philogyny [fi-läj´-ä-nē] fondness for women

philology [fi-läl´-ə-jē] study of a culture's language and literature [literally, a fondness for words]

phob   fear

acrophobia [ak´-rə-fō´-bē-ə] abnormal fear of high places

bibliophobia [bib´-lē-ə-fō´-bē-ə] dread or hatred of books

cardiophobia [kär´-dē-ə-fō´-bē-ə] abnormal fear of heart disease

gynophobia [jin´-ə-fō´-bē-ə] fear of women

hydrophobia [hī´-drə-fō´-bē-ə] fear of water

ideophobia [īdēə´-fō´-bē-ə] fear or distrust of ideas

kleptophobia [klep´-tə-fō´-bē-ə] fear of stealing [or being stolen from]

monophobia [män´-ə-fō´-bē-ə] abnormal fear of being alone

neophobia [nē´-ə-fō´-bē-ə] fear of change or new thing

phonophobia [fō´-nə-fō´-bē-ə] fear of sound or speaking

xenophobia [zen´-ə-fō´-bē-ə] fear of strangers

phon   sound

antiphony [an-tif´-ə-nē] opposition of sounds between two groups

bronchophony [brän´-käf´-ə-nē] sound of the voice heard through the stethoscope over healthy lungs (Medical)

cacophony [kə-käf´-ə-nē] harsh sound, dissonance

euphony [yoo´-fə-ne] pleasing or sweet sound

homophonic [häm´-ə-fän´-ik] having the same sound

phonic [fän´-ik] related to sound

polyphonic [päl´-i-fän´-ik] having many sounds (Music)

symphonic [sim-fän´-ik] related to the combining or harmony of sounds

telephonic [tel´-ə-fän´-ik] related

to transmission of sound from a distance

phone   sound

hydrophone [hī´-drə-fōn´] receiver for listening to sound transmitted through water

ideophone [ī´-dē-ə-fōn´] sound or pattern of sounds used to represent a concept

optophone [äp´-tə-fōn´] device used by the visually impaired to convert written text into sounds

telegraphone [ti-leg´-rə-fōn] early device for recording sound

telephone [tel´-ə-fōn´] a device that transmits sound from a distance

phono   sound

phonogenic [fō´-nə-jen´-ik] suitable for producing sound

phonogram [fō´-nə-gram´] letter or symbol that represents a sound

phonology [fō-näl´-ə-jē] study of speech sounds

phonometer [fō-näm´-ə-tər] instrument which measures the intensity of sound

phonopathy [fə-näp´-ə-thē] speech disorder

phonophile [fō´-nə-fīl´] lover and collector of phonograph records

phonophobia [fō´-nə-fō´-bē-ə] fear of sound or speaking

phonoscope [fō´-nə-skōp´] instrument which represents sound vibrations in a visible form

pod   foot

bipod [bī´-päd´] two-legged support

polypod [päl´-i-päd´] having many feet

tripod [trī´-päd] three-legged stand

podo   foot

pododermatitis [pä-dō-dūr´-mə-tīt´-is] inflammation of the skin tissue of the foot

podology [pä-däl´-ə-jē] study of the physiology of the feet (Medical)

poly (combining form) many

polyandry [päl´-ē-an´-drē] practice of having two or more husbands at one time

polyarchy [pä´-lē-är´-kē] rule by many

polycentric [päl'-i-sen´-trik] having more than one center (Biology); having multiple centers of control (Political Science)

polychrome [päl´-i-krōm´] many-colored

polygamy [pə-lig´-ə-mē] having more than one spouse at the same time

polygenic [päl´-i-jen´-ik] coming from multiple genes (Biology)

polyonymous [päl´-ē-än´-ə-mäs] having many names

polyphonic [päl´-i-fän´-ik] having many sounds (Music)

polypod [päl´-i-päd´] having many feet

polytheism [päl´-i-thē´-iz´-m] belief in many gods

pseud false

pseudonym [sōo´-də-nim´] fictitious name, especially one assumed by an author

psych mind, spirit

psychosis [sī-kō´-sis] condition of mental illness

psycho mind, spirit

psychobiology [sī´-kō-bī-äl´-ə-jē] study of relationship between biological processes and behavior

psychogenic [sī´-kō-jen´-ik] originating in the mind

psychograph [sī´-kə-graf´] chart of an individual's personality traits

psychology [sī-käl´-ə-jē] science of the mind

psychometric [sī´-kə- met´-rik] related to the measurement of mental data

psychonomic [sī´-kə-näm´-ik] related to laws of behavior and cognitive function

psychopathology [sī´-kō-pa-thäl´-ə-jē] study of mental illness

psychosomatic [sī´-kō-sō-mat´-ik] related to the effect of the mind on the body (Medical)

psychotheism [sī´-kō-thē´-iz-m] doctrine that God is pure spirit

scop look at, view, examine

macroscopic [mak´-rə-skäp´-ik] visible to the naked eye

microscopic [mī´-krə-skäp´-ik] too small to be seen by the naked eye

scope look at, view, examine

bronchoscope [brän´-kə-skōp´] thin tube which enables a doctor to see into the airways

cardioscope [kär´-dē-ə-skōp´] instrument for viewing the interior of the heart

chromoscope [krō´-mə-skōp´] optical instrument used to study various properties of color, including value and intensity

helioscope [hē´-lē-ə-skōp´] device for viewing the sun

hydroscope [hī´-drə-skōp´] device for viewing objects below the surface of water

periscope [per´-ə-skōp´] instrument for viewing surrounding area, especially objects not in the direct line of sight

phonoscope [fō´-nə-skōp´] instrument which represents sound vibrations in a visible form

telescope [tel´-ə-skōp´] instrument which makes distant objects appear nearer and larger

somat body

mesosomatic [me-zō´-sō-mat´-ik] related to the middle region of the body of various invertebrates (Zoology)

psychosomatic [sī´-kō-sō-mat´-ik] related to the effect of the mind on the body (Medical)

somato   body

somatogenic [sō´-mə-tə-jen´-ik] originating in the cells of the body (Medical)

somatology [sō´-mə-täl´-ə-jē] study of human physical characteristics (Anthropology)

somatometry [sō´-mə-täm´-ə-trē] related to body measurement (Anthropology)

taph   tomb

epitaph [ep´-ə-taf´] inscription on a tomb or gravestone

tele   (combining form) from afar

telegram [tel´-ə-gram´] written message sent from a distance

telegraphone [ti-leg´-rə-fōn] early device for recording sound

telemetry [tə-lem´-ə-trē] measurement of the distance of an object from an observer

telepathy [tə-lep´-ə-thē] communication between minds

telephone [tel´-ə-fōn´] device that transmits sound from a distance

telephonic [tel´-ə-fän´-ik] relating to transmission of sound from a distance

telescope [tel´-ə-skōp´] instrument which makes distant objects appear nearer and larger

telethermometry [tel´-ə-thər-mäm´-ə-trē] process for taking remote temperature measurements

thanas   death

euthanasia [yoo´-thə-na´-zhə] good death, easy and painless death

the   god

atheism [ā´-thē-iz´-m] denial of the existence of a god

monotheism [män´-ə-thē´-iz´-m] belief in one god

polytheism [päl´-i-thē´-iz´-m] belief in many gods

psychotheism [sī´-kō-thē´-iz´-m] doctrine that God is pure spirit

theo   god

theology [thē-äl´-ə-jē] study of the nature of God

theonomy [thē-ä´-nə-me] governed by a god; divine rule

theopathy [thē-äp´-ə-thē] intense absorption in religious devotion

therap   treatment

hydrotherapy [hī´-drō-ther´-ə-pē] treatment of disease of injury by the use of baths, etc.

therm   heat

chronothermal [krä´-nä-thūr´ m´l] relating to both time and temperature

diathermy [dī´-ə-thūr´-mē] generation of heat in body tissue by electric current (Medical)

geothermal [jē´-ō-thūr´-m´l] related to the heat of the earth's interior

hydrothermal [hī´-drō-thūr´-məl] of or relating to hot water

hypothermia [hī´-pə-thūr´-mē-ə] condition of reduced temperature

isothermal [ī´-sə-thūr´-m´l] related to equality or constancy of temperature

mesotherm [mez´-ō-thərm´] plant that requires a moderate degree of heat (Biology)

thermal [thūr´-m´l] of or related to heat, caused by heat

thermo   heat

telethermometry [tel´-ə-thər-mäm´-ə-trē] process for taking remote temperature measurements

thermogenic [thūr´-mə-jen´-ik] producing heat (Physiology)

thermography [thər-mäg´-rə-fē] recording a visual image of body heat using infrared devices (Medical)

thermometer [thər-mäm´-ə-tər] instrument which measures heat

xeno   foreign, strange

xenophile [zen´-ə-fīl´] lover of foreign things

xenophobia [zen´-ə fō´-bē-ə] fear of strangers

GREEK AND LATIN SUFFIXES

-ac   Greek — related to, pertaining to
cardiac [kär´-dē-ak´] pertaining to the heart

-ad   Latin — group
myriad [mir´-ē-əd] too numerous to count; innumerable

-al   Latin — like, related to; an action or process
chronothermal [krô´-nä-thūr´-m'l] relating to both time and temperature
epidermal [ep´-ə-dūr´-m'l] related to the outer layer of skin (Biology)
geothermal [jē´-ō-thūr´-m'l] related to the heat of the earth's interior
hydrothermal [hī´-drō-thūr´-məl] of or relating to hot water
isothermal [ī´-sə-thūr´-m'l] related to equality or constancy of temperature
nautical [nôt´-i-kəl] related to ships or sailing
optical [äp´-ti-kəl] pertaining to the eye, vision
pericardial [per´-ə-kär´-dē'l] situated around the heart (Biology)
thermal [thūr´-m'l] of or related to heat, caused by heat

-ant   Latin — one who, that which; state, quality
hydrant [hī´-drənt] device for drawing water

-ate   Latin — to make, to act; one who, that which
dehydrate [dē-hī´-drāt] to take water from

-cide   Latin — kill
genocide [jen´-ə-sīd´] killing of a race

-er   Latin — one who, that which
geographer [jē-äg´-rə-fər] one who writes about the earth's features
nomographer [nō-mäg´-rə-fər] writer of laws

-esis   Greek — action, process
genesis [jen´-ə-sis] coming into being
neogenesis [nē´-ō-jen´-ə-sis] new formation (as of tissue)

-ia   Greek — condition
acrophobia [ak´-rə-fō´-bē-ə] an abnormal fear of high places
bibliomania [bib´-lē-ə-mā´-nē-ə] excessive preoccupation with books
bibliophobia [bib´-lē-ə-fō´-bē-ə] dread or hatred of books
cardiophobia [kär´-dē-ə-fō´-bē-ə] abnormal fear of heart disease
euthanasia [yoo´-thə-na´-zhə] good death, easy and painless death
graphomania [graf´-ə-mā´-nē-ə] obsessive desire to write
gynophobia [gin´-ə-fō´-bē-ə] fear of women
hydrophobia [hī´-drə-fō´-bē-ə] fear of water
hyperchromia [hī´-pər-krō´-mē-ə] excessive pigmentation [color], as of the skin
hypochromia [hī´-pə-krō´-mē-ə] lack of color
hypomania [hī´-pə-mā´-nē-ə] mild form of psychosis indicated by an elevated mood
hypothermia [hī´-pə-thūr´-mē-ə] condition of reduced temperature
ideophobia [īd´-ēə-fō´-bē-ə] fear or distrust of ideas
kleptomania [klep´-tə-mā´-nē-ə] persistent craving to steal
kleptophobia [klep´-tə-fō´-bē-ə] fear of stealing (or being stolen from)
monomania [män´-ə-mā´-nē-ə] obsession with one object or idea
monophobia [män´-ə-fō´-bē-ə] abnormal fear of being alone
neophobia [nē´-ə-fō´-bē-ə] fear of change or new things
phonophobia [fō´-nə-fō´-bē-ə] fear of sound or speaking
xenophobia [zen´-ə-fō´-bē-ə] fear of strangers

-ic   Latin — like, related to
androcentric [an´-drō-sen´-trik] centered around male interests
anthropopathic [an´-thrə-pō-path´-ik] relating human feelings to something not human
antisymmetric [an-ti-si-met´-rik] having opposite and irregular properties

bicentric [bī´-sen´-trik] related to a classification of plant or animal with two centers of origin (Biology)

biogenic [bī´-ō-jen´-ik] produced by the action of living organisms (Geology)

bronchogenic [brän´-kō-jen´-ik] originating from the air passages of the lungs (Medical)

chromogenic [krō´-mə-jen´-ik] producing color

chronic [krän´-ik] continuing a long time or recurring frequently

cyclic [sī´-klik] occurring or repeating in cycles

cyclogenic [sī´-klä-jen´-ik] relating to life cycles

diachronic [dī´-ə-krän´-ik] considering phenomena, such as languages, as they change over time

diadermic [dī´-ə-dər´-mik] acting through the skin

eugenic [yoo-jen´-ik] of good birth

geocentric [jē´-ō-sen´ trik] related to the earth's center; earth-centered

gynecocentric [gīn-ə´-kō-sen´-trik] centered around the female point of view

gynecogenic [gīn-ə´-kō-jen´-ik] causing female characteristics

heliocentric [hē´-lē-ō-sen´-trik] centered on the sun

homophonic [häm´-ə-fän´-ik] having the same sound

hydrogenic [hī´-drə-jen´-ik] caused by the action of water (Geology)

hypodermic [hī´-pə-dūr´-mik] under the skin

logic [läj´-ik] related to theory of reasoning (Philosophy)

macroscopic [mak´-rə-skäp´-ik] visible to the naked eye

mesodermic [mes´-ə-dūr´-mik] related to the middle layer of skin (Biology)

mesophilic [mez´-ə-fil´-ik] thriving in a moderate environment (Biology)

mesosomatic [mez-ō´-sō-mat´-ik] related to the middle region of the body of various invertebrates (Zoology)

metric [met´-rik] related to the system of meters

microscopic [mī´-krə-skäp´-ik] too small to be seen by the naked eye

monocentric [mä´-nə-sen´-trik] having a single center

monogenic [män´-ə-jen´-ik] having a single or common origin

monophonic [män´-ə-fän´-ik] having one sound

nautical [nôt´-i-kəl] related to ships or sailing

neoanthropic [nē´-ō-an-thräp´-ik] belonging to the same species as recent man

neocosmic [nē´-ō-käz´-mik] related to the universe in its present state

optical [äp´-ti-kəl] pertaining to the eye, vision

Paleolithic [pā´-lē-ə-lith´-ik] related to the early Stone Age

pandemic [pan-dem´-ik] having a widespread effect on the population

pathogenic [path´-ə-jen´-ik] causing disease

perioptic [per´-ē-äp´-tik] situated about or surrounding the eyeball (Medical)

phonic [fän´-ik] relating to sound

phonogenic [fō´-nə-jen´-ik] suitable for producing sound

polycentric [päl'-i-sen´-trik] having more than one center (Biology); having multiple centers of control (Political Science)

polygenic [päl´-i-jen´-ik] coming from multiple genes

polyphonic [päl´-i-fän´-ik] having many sounds (Music)

psychogenic [sī´-kō-jen´-ik] originating in the mind

psychometric [sī´-kə-met´-rik] related to the measurement of mental processes

psychonomic [sī´-kə-näm´-ik] related to laws of behavior and cognitive function

psychosomatic [sī´-kō-sō-mat´-ik] related to the effect of the mind on the body (Medical)

somatogenic [sō´-mə-tə-jen´-ik] originating in the cells of the body (Medical)

symmetric [si-met´-rik] having corresponding parts the same in size and form

symphonic [sim-fän´-ik] related to a harmony of sounds

synoptic [si-näp´-tik] taking a general view of the whole subject
telephonic [tel´-ə-fän´-ik] relating to transmission of sound from a distance
thermogenic [thŭr´-mə-jen´-ik] producing heat (Physiology)

-ics   Latin — science, related to, system
astronautics [as´-trə-nôt´-iks] technology of spacecraft design and building
hydronautics [hī´-drə-nôt´-iks] related to the development of deep submersible vehicles

-ism   Latin — act, state, condition
anachronism [ə-nak´-rə-niz´-m] something out of place or time
atheism [ā´-thē-iz´-m] denial of the existence of a god
misoneism [mis´-ō-nē´-iz´-m] hatred of innovation or change
monotheism [män´-ə-thē´-iz´-m] belief in one god
neologism [nē-äl´-ə-jiz´-m] new word or phrase
neogenesis [nē´-ō-jen´-ə-sis] new formation [as of tissue]
polytheism [päl´-i-thē´-iz´-m] belief in many gods
psychotheism [sī´-kō-thē´-iz´-m] doctrine that God is pure spirit

-ist   Latin — one who
misogamist [mi-säg´-ə-məst] one who hates marriage
misologist [mi-säl´-ə-jist] one who hates reasoning

-itis   Greek — inflammation
arthritis [är-thrit´-is] inflammation of the joint
bronchitis [brän-kīt´-is] inflammation of the air passages
dermatitis [dŭr´-mə-tī´-tis] inflammation of the skin
encephalitis [en-sef´-ə-lī´-tis] inflamma-tion of the brain
pododermatitis [pä-dō-dŭr´-mə-tīt´-is] inflammation of skin tissue of the foot

-ium   Latin — chemical element
chromium [krō´-mē-əm] element used for making pigments

-logy   Greek — study of, science
anthropology [an´-thrə-päl´-ə-jē] study of mankind
astrogeology [as´-trə-jē-äl´-ə-jē] study of the structure and composition of heavenly bodies
astrology [a-sträl´-ə-jē] study of the influence of the stars on humans
bibliology [bib´-lē-äl´-ə-jē] history and science of books as physical objects
cardiology [kär´-dē-äl´-ə-jē] study of the heart
chronology [krə-näl´-ə-jē] science of determining the order in which things occur
dermatology [dŭr´-mə-täl´-ə-jē] study of the skin
geochronology [jē´-ō-krə-näl´-ə-jē] study of the ages of geologic events
geology [jē-äl´-ə-jē] study of the earth's structure
geopathology [jē´-äl-path-äl-ə-jē] study of the relationship between diseases and specific geographic locations
graphology [graf-äl´-ə-jē] study of handwriting
gynecology [gī´-nä-käl´-ə-jē] science of women's disorders (Medical)
hydrogeology [hī´-drə-jē-äl´-ə-jē] study of subsurface water movement through rocks
ideology [ī´-dē-äl´-ə-jē] system of interrelated social beliefs and values
metrology [me-träl´-ə-jē] science of weights and measures
microbiology [mī´-krō-bī-äl´-ə-jē] study of minute forms of life
nomology [nō-mäl´-ə-jē] science of laws and lawmaking (Philosophy)
pathology [pə-thäl´-ə-jē] study of disease
phonology [fō-näl´-ə-jē] study of speech sounds
podology [pə-däl´-ə-jē] study of physiology of the feet (Medical)
psychobiology [sī´-kō-bī-äl´-ə-jē] study of relationship between biological processes and behavior
psychology [sī-käl´-ə-jē] science of the mind
psychopathology [sī´-kō-pa-thäl´-ə-jē] study of mental illness

somatology [sō´-mə-tāl´-ə-jē] study of human physical characteristics (Anthropology)

theology [thē-āl´-ə-jē] study of the nature of God

-oid   Greek — resembling

android [an´-droid] humanlike robot

anthropoid [an´-thrə-poid´] resembling man

dermoid [dūr´-moid] resembling skin (Medical)

gynecoid [gin´-ə-koid´] physically resembling the female

-ology   Greek — study of, science

entomology [en´-tə-māl´-ə-jē] branch of zoology that deals with insects

hematology [hē´-mə-tāl´-ə-jē] study of blood and its diseases (Medical)

-on   Greek — quality, state

anthelion [ant´-hēl´-y-ən] bright spot opposite the sun

perihelion [per´-ə-hē´-lē-ən) point closest to the sun in a planet's orbit (Astronomy)

-osis   Greek — condition

dermatosis [dūr´-mə-tō´-sis] disease of the skin

psychosis [sī-kō´-sis] condition of mental illness

-ous   Latin— having the quality of

amorphous [ə-môr´-fəs] without definite form, shapeless

amphibious [am-fib´-ē-əs] able to live on both land and water

androgynous [an-dräj´-ə-nəs] having both male and female characteristics

anonymous [ə-nän´-ə-məs] without a name

autogenous [ô-tāj´-ə-nəs] produced from within, self-generating (Biology)

autonomous [ô-tän´-ə-məs] self-governing, subject to one's own laws

exogenous [ek-sāj-ə-nəs] caused by a factor or agent outside the organism (Medical)

geogenous [jē´-āj´-ə-nəs] growing on or in the ground

hypogenous [hī-pāj´-ə-nəs] growing on the underside (Botany)

hypogeous [hī'-pə-jē´-əs] happening underground (Geology)

monogynous [mə-näj´-ə-nəs] having

only one wife at a time

onymous [än´-ə-məs] having the writer's name

polyonymous [pāl´-ē-än´-ə-məs] having many names

synchronous [sin´-krə-nəs] occurring at the same time

synonymous [si-nän´-ə-məs] having a similar meaning

-sis   Greek — action, process

antibiosis [an´-ti-bī-ō´-sis] association between organisms which is injurious to one of them

macrobiosis [mak´-rō-bī´-ō´-sis] longevity

symbiosis [sim´-bī-ō´-sis] living together

-y   Greek — state of, quality, act; body, group

agronomy [ə-grän´-ə-mē] management of farm land

anarchy [an´-ər-kē] absence of rule

androcracy [an´-dräk´-rə-sē] political and social rule by men

anthroponomy [an´-thrə-pän´-ə-mē] natural laws of human development as they relate to the environment

antilogy [an-til´-ə-jē] contradiction in terms or ideas

antinomy [an-tin´-ə-mē] opposition of one law to another

antipathy [an-tip´-ə-thē] feeling of dislike or opposition towards something

antiphony [an-tif´-ə-nē] opposition of sounds between two groups

antisymmetry [an´-ti-si´-met-rē] opposing, irregular properties

apathy [ap´-ə-thē] lack of feeling

astrography [ə-sträg´-rə-fē] mapping of the planets and stars

astrometry [ə-sträm´-ə-trē] measurement of the positions and distances of stars

astronomy [ə-strän´-ə-mē] science dealing with the order of celestial bodies

autobiography [ôt´-ə-bī-ä´-grə-fē] person's life story written by himself

autocracy [ô-tä´-krə-sē] rule by one person with unlimited power

bibliography [bib´-lē-äg´-rə-fē] list of books

biography [bī-äg´-rə-fē] written story of someone's life

biometry [bī-äm´-ə-trē] statistical analysis of biological observations and phenomena

biopsy [bī´-äp'-sē] removal and examination of tissue from a living body

bronchophony [brän´-käf´-ə-nē] sound of the voice heard through the stethoscope over healthy lungs (Medical)

cacophony [kə-käf´-ə-nē] harsh sound, dissonance

cardiopathy [kär´-dē-äp´-ə-thē] disease of the heart

diathermy [dī´-ə-thūr´-mē] generation of heat in body tissue by electric current (Medical)

entomology [en´-tə-mäl´-ə-jē] branch of zoology that deals with insects

eulogy [yoo´-lə-jē] speech in praise of someone

eunomy [yoo´-nə-mē] civil order under good laws; good government

euphony [yoo´-fə-nē] pleasing or sweet sound

geochrony [jē´-äk´-rə-nē] system of time divisions used in the study of the earth

geography [jē-äg´-rə-fē] description of the earth's features

geopathology [jē´-äl-path-äl-ə-jē] study of the relationship between diseases and specific geographic locations

gynarchy [gin´-är´-kē] rule by women

gynocracy [gi´-näk´-rə-sē] government by women

hydronymy [hī-drän´-ə-mē] naming or names of bodies of water

hydropathy [hī-dräp´-ə-thē] treatment of injury or disease with water (Medical)

hydrotherapy [hī´-drō-ther´-ə-pē] treatment of disease or injury by the use of baths, etc.

ideocracy [īd-ē´-äk´-rə-sē] government based on an all-embracing idea or theory

ideogeny [īd´-ē-äj´-ə-nē] origin of ideas (Philosophy)

lithography [li-thäg´-rə-fē] process of printing from a metal (originally stone) plate

mesocracy [mä-zäk´-rə-sē] government by the middle classes

misogyny [mi-säj´-ə-nē] hatred of women

monarchy [män´-ər-kē] rule by one person

neocracy [nē´-äk´-rä-sē] government by those new to government

neography [nē-äg´-rə-fē] new system or method of writing

optometry [äp-täm´-ə-trē] testing of eyes to measure vision

philanthropy [fi-lan´-thrə-pē] love of mankind

philogyny [fi-läj´-ə-nē] fondness for women

philology [fi-läl´-ə-jē] study of a culture's language and literature [literally, a fondness for words]

phonopathy [fə-näp´-ə-thē] speech disorder

polyandry [päl´-ē-an´-drē] practice of having two or more husbands at one time

polyarchy [pä´-lē-är´-kē] rule by many

polygamy [pä-lig´-ə-mē] having more than one spouse at the same time

somatometry [so´-mə-täm´-ə-tre] related to body measurement (Anthropology)

sympathy [sim´-pä-thē] supporting another's viewpoint, ability to share another's feelings

synarchy [sin´-ər-kē] joint rule

telemetry [tə-lem´-ə-trē] measurement of the distance of an object from an observer

telepathy [tə-lep´-ə-thē] communication between minds

telethermometry [tel´-ə-thər-mäm´-ə-trē] process for taking remote temperature measurements

theonomy [thē-ä´-nə-mē] governed by a god; divine rule

theopathy [thē-äp´-ə-thē] intense absorption in religious devotion

thermography [thär-mäg´-rä-fē] recording a visual image of body heat using infrared devices (Medical)

triarchy [tri´-är-kē] rule or government by three persons